4 Habits

Quiet Time ~ Gratitude
Service ~ Exercise

By Josh Hunt

Contents

4 Habits, Lesson #1
Hebrews 10.24, 25
The Power of Habits
Good Questions Have Groups Talking
www.joshhunt.com

OPEN

What is your name and one habit you wish you could stop or start.

DIG

1. **Hebrews 10.24, 25. What do we learn about Christian living from this passage? There can be numerous right answers.**

    I LIKE THE STORY of the little boy who fell out of bed. When his Mom asked him what happened, he answered, "I don't know. I guess I stayed too close to where I got in."

    Easy to do the same with our faith. It's tempting just to stay where we got in and never move.

    Pick a time in the not-too-distant past. A year or two ago. Now ask yourself a few questions. How does your prayer life today compare with then? How about your giving? Have both the amount and the joy increased? What about your church loyalty? Can you tell you've grown? And Bible study? Are you learning to learn?

- We will in all things grow up into him who is the Head, that is, Christ. (Eph. 4:15 NIV, emphasis mine)

- Let us leave the elementary teachings about Christ and go on to maturity. (Heb. 6:1 NIV, emphasis mine)

- Like newborn babies, crave pure spiritual milk, so that by it you may grow up in your salvation. (1 Pet. 2:2 NIV, emphasis mine)

- But grow in the grace and knowledge of our Lord and Savior Jesus Christ. (2 Pet. 3:18 NIV, emphasis mine)

Growth is the goal of the Christian. Maturity is mandatory. If a child ceased to develop, the parent would be concerned, right? Doctors would be called. Tests would be run. When a child stops growing, something is wrong.

When a Christian stops growing, help is needed. If you are the same Christian you were a few months ago, be careful. You might be wise to get a checkup. Not on your body, but on your heart. Not a physical, but a spiritual.

May I suggest one?

At the risk of sounding like a preacher—which is what I am—may I make a suggestion? Why don't you check your habits? Though there are many bad habits, there are also many good ones. In fact, I can find four in the Bible. Make these four habits regular activities and see what happens. — Max Lucado, *When God Whispers Your Name* (Dallas: Word Pub., 1994), 135–136.

2. **Why had the people mentioned in this passage quit coming to church? Had they rebelled against God? Had they become atheists?**

They just got out of the habit.

3. **How would you define this word, habit? What is a habit and why are they important?**

ἔθος, ους n; ἦθος, ους n; συνήθεια, ας f: a pattern of behavior more or less fixed by tradition and generally sanctioned by the society—'custom, habit.' — Johannes P. Louw and Eugene Albert Nida, *Greek-English Lexicon of the New Testament: Based on Semantic Domains* (New York: United Bible Societies, 1996), 506.

A HABIT is like an invisible thread, but every time we repeat the act we strengthen the strand, add to it another filament, until it becomes a great cable that binds us irrevocably through thought and act. ORRISON SWETT MARDEN / Zig Ziglar, *Inspiration from the Top: A Collection of My Favorite Quotes* (Nashville: Thomas Nelson, 2012).

4. **Do you think about whether you are going to come to church, or is it a habit?**

Help yourself by developing godly habits (e.g., daily Bible reading, regular church attendance, fellowship with other believers, helping others). When stressed, people revert to old habits—even good ones. For a semester, researchers collected data on a group of undergraduates' eating, exercise, and other behaviors. When students were sleep-deprived, they were more likely to stick to old habits. Students who ate unhealthy pastries or doughnuts for breakfast ate even more during exams. Similarly, people who went to the gym were more likely to go to the gym when stressed. If you are in the habit of reading your Bible you are more likely to keep doing that even in a crisis. — Edward E. Moody, *Surviving Culture: When Character and Your World Collide* (Nashville: Randall House, 2014).

5. How much of our lives is habit? How much of our lives is on autopilot?

I have read that as much as 40 percent of everything we do is done merely from habit. If you are reading this book it is probably because you have formed a habit of frequent reading. Others who desperately need the information contained in this book won't get it simply because they have not formed a habit of reading. They probably say, "I hate to read." If you repeatedly say you hate a thing, it only makes it harder to do and less enjoyable. Good habits can be developed, and any bad habit can be broken through repetition. The experts say that a habit can be formed or broken in thirty days, so I am inviting you to give it a try and change your life by changing your habits. At first it may be difficult, but diligence and patience will eventually make you succeed. One of the reasons we don't develop the good habits we say we want is because we live in a culture of instant gratification. We want everything now and don't realize that many of the good things we want and need are not attained just because we want them. Good habits come to those who are persistent and refuse to quit. Vince Lombardi said, "Winning is a habit; unfortunately, so is losing." He also said, "Once you learn to quit, it becomes a habit." Make a decision right now that you can and will be a winner at forming any good habit you want to form and breaking any bad habit that you want to break.

— Making Good Habits, Breaking Bad Habits: 14 New Behaviors That Will Energize Your Life by Joyce Meyer

6. How do we get rid of bad habits?

By developing good ones. Here are four to start with:

First, the habit of prayer: "Base your happiness on your hope in Christ. When trials come endure them patiently; steadfastly maintain the habit of prayer" (Rom. 12:12 PHILLIPS, emphasis mine). Posture, tone, and place are personal matters. Select the form that works for you. But don't think about it too much. Better to pray awkwardly than not at all.

Second, the habit of study: "The man who looks into the perfect mirror of God's law . . . and makes a habit of so doing, is not the man who sees and forgets. He puts that law into practice and he wins true happiness" (James 1:25 PHILLIPS, emphasis mine).

Third, the habit of giving: "On every Lord's Day each of you should put aside something from what you have earned during the week, and use it for this offering. The amount depends on how much the Lord has helped you earn" (1 Cor. 16:2 TLB, emphasis mine). You don't give for God's sake. You give for your sake. "The purpose of tithing is to teach you always to put God first in your lives" (Deut. 14:23 TLB).

And last of all, the habit of fellowship: "Let us not give up the habit of meeting together, as some are doing. Instead, let us encourage one another" (Heb. 10:25 TEV, emphasis mine). You need support. You need what the Bible calls fellowship. And you need it every week.

Four habits worth having. Isn't it good to know that some habits are good for you? — Max Lucado, *Max on Life: Answers and Inspiration for Today's Questions* (Nashville: Thomas Nelson, 2011).

7. How do we cultivate good habits?

The key to developing almost any habit comes down to this:

- Set a low bar

- Go for ruthless consistency

Set a low bar—don't try to read through the Bible in a year at first. Get the Book open every day. There is a verse in Nehemiah that says that, "Ezra opened the book..." This is the key to life-changing Bible study. Open the Book. Open it every day. You don't have to read a lot. You do have to do it every day. Go for ruthless consistency. Don't allow any exceptions. Get the Book open every single day. — Josh Hunt, *The Habit of Discipleship* (Pulpit Press, 2015).

8. Let's consider how we can spur one another on to form good habits. How can we help each other form good habits?

The Bible teaches what science in just now learning. The Bible says, "Walk with the wise and become wise, for a companion of fools suffers harm." Proverbs 13:20 (NIV2011) Wisdom is contagious and stupid is contagious. Almost everything is contagious. If you are a 16 year old girl and your unwed 18-year-old sister gets pregnant, you are more likely to get pregnant. If you struggle with weight (who doesn't?) and your friend gains weight, you are more likely to gain weight. In fact, if your friend's friend gains weight—a person you don't even know—the odds go up that you will gain weight.

Behavior is contagious, as this story illustrates.

On a fall morning in 1998, a teacher at a Tennessee high school noticed the smell of gas in her classroom and soon felt dizzy and nauseous. Some of her students then reported feeling ill as well, and they were transported by ambulance to a nearby hospital. As concerned staff and students watched them go, some of them started feeling sick, too.

That day, 100 people showed up in the emergency room with symptoms they believed to be associated with the exposure to gas at the school. But the illnesses could not be explained by medical tests. Extensive environmental tests conducted at the school concluded that no toxic source could be the cause, according to results published in the New England Journal of Medicine.

What occurred was real illness, although not caused by germs or fumes, according to Timothy F. Jones, lead author of the paper and deputy state epidemiologist at the Tennessee Department of Health.

"It was not an infection, but it was certainly transmitted," Jones said.

It was a phenomenon known as mass psychogenic illness, in which symptoms are passed from person to person among people who are visible to one another.

"You get sick because you see someone else getting sick," said Jones.

Mass psychogenic illness is an extreme example of the more general phenomenon of contagious behavior: the unconscious transmission of actions or emotions from one individual to another.

Behavior is contagious. If you hang around godly people, you are more likely to become godly. If you hang around scripture-memorizing people, you are more likely to memorize scripture. If you hang around praying people, you are more likely to pray.

It is not enough to be in the same room. It is not enough to sit on straight rows and watch the same events on the same stage. We must interact. We must talk. We must listen. We must connect. — Josh Hunt, *Transformed By...*

9. **In this series, we will look at four discipleship habits. I'd like for us to preview each of these today. First: start your day with your Bible on your lap. What good things come to those who start their day with their Bible on their lap?**

I've learned that serving the Lord requires prayer, and often means tears....

Any day that I leave my room without a quiet time with God, I look for the devil to hit me from every angle. Power for life, for ministry, doesn't come from our own ability; it comes from God. We need a fresh, daily anointing from the Holy Spirit, and that comes from the time we spend with God in His Word and in prayer. Are you a person of prayer?

In Boston, Massachusetts, the great soul winner John Vassar knocked on the door of a person's home and asked the woman if she knew Christ as her Savior. She replied, "It's none of your business" and slammed the door in his face. He stood on the doorstep and wept and wept, and she looked out her window and saw him weeping. The next Sunday she was in church. She said it was because of those tears. Where are your tears?

A life fueled by prayer and characterized by His love is a life God will use. — Billy Graham, *Wisdom for Each Day* (Nashville: Thomas Nelson, 2008).

10. What are we missing if we are not in the habit of a daily quiet time in the Word and prayer?

I can summarize Christian living as one habit: the habit of the Quiet Time. There is much that will come after this—service and evangelism and all kinds of character development. But, it all flows out of the time alone with God in prayer and in His Word. — Josh Hunt, *The Habit of Discipleship* (Pulpit Press, 2015).

11. The second habit is gratitude. Same two questions. First, what good things come to the grateful?

Yes, "thank you" is an essential, everyday part of family dinners, trips to the store, business deals, and political negotiations. That might be why so many people have dismissed gratitude as simple, obvious, and unworthy of serious attention.

But that's starting to change. Recently scientists have begun to chart a course of research aimed at understanding gratitude and the circumstances in which it flourishes or diminishes. They're finding that people who practice gratitude consistently report a host of benefits:

Stronger immune systems and lower blood pressure;

Higher levels of positive emotions;

More joy, optimism, and happiness;

Acting with more generosity and compassion;

Feeling less lonely and isolated.

12. What pain do the ungrateful bring upon themselves?

It's that time of year where many people begin thinking about everything they have to be thankful for. Although it's nice to count your blessings on Thanksgiving, being thankful throughout the year could have tremendous benefits on your quality of life.

In fact, gratitude may be one of the most overlooked tools that we all have access to every day. Cultivating gratitude doesn't cost any money and it certainly doesn't take much time, but the benefits are enormous. Research reveals gratitude can have these seven benefits:

1. Gratitude opens the door to more relationships. Not only does saying "thank you" constitute good manners, but showing appreciation can help you win new friends, according to a 2104 study published in Emotion. The study found that thanking a new acquaintance makes them more likely to seek an ongoing relationship. So whether you thank a stranger for holding the door or you send a quick thank-you note to that co-worker who helped you with a project, acknowledging other people's contributions can lead to new opportunities.

2. Gratitude improves physical health. Grateful people experience fewer aches and pains and they report feeling healthier than other people, according to a 2012 study published in Personality and Individual Differences. Not surprisingly, grateful people are also more likely to take care of their health. They exercise more often and are more likely to attend regular check-ups with their doctors, which is likely to contribute to further longevity.

3. Gratitude improves psychological health. Gratitude reduces a multitude of toxic emotions, ranging from envy and resentment to frustration and regret. Robert A. Emmons, Ph.D., a leading gratitude researcher, has conducted multiple studies on the link between gratitude and well-being. His research confirms that gratitude effectively increases happiness and reduces depression. http://www.forbes.com/sites/amymorin/2014/11/23/7-scientifically-proven-benefits-of-gratitude-that-will-motivate-you-to-give-thanks-year-round/#556f6a656800

13. Quick! Quick! Let's each list three thing we are grateful for. No repeats.

Rejoicing is not an easy task. It is one of the most difficult things you will ever put your mind to. A good way to start is with the activity of gratitude. There are a million ways you can practice gratitude. One thing I often do is make a list of twenty things I am grateful for before I go to bed each night:

- Five family members I am grateful for

- Five other people I am grateful for

- Five physical things I am grateful for

- Five spiritual things I am grateful for.

Over time, gratitude stats to change your mind. The Bible says we are transformed by the renewing of our mind, not by trying really hard to be good. One way to transform the mind is to practice the activity of gratitude. Paul did. He made it a habit to thank God every time he thought of his friends in Philippi. I wonder what else he was in the habit of thanking God for.

Gratitude paves the way to joy. — Josh Hunt, *Pure Joy*, 2013.

14. **What were the first two habits? Third is service. It has to do with doing some small act of unselfishness every day. What good would come our way if we made this a habit?**

Volunteering provides many benefits to both mental and physical health.

Volunteering helps counteract the effects of stress, anger, and anxiety. The social contact aspect of helping and working with others can have a profound effect on your overall psychological well-being. Nothing relieves stress better than a meaningful connection to another person. Working with pets and other animals has also been shown to improve mood and reduce stress and anxiety.

Volunteering combats depression. Volunteering keeps you in regular contact with others and helps you develop a solid support system, which in turn protects you against depression.

Volunteering makes you happy. By measuring hormones and brain activity, researchers have discovered that being helpful to others delivers immense pleasure. Human beings are hard-wired to give to others. The more we give, the happier we feel.

Volunteering increases self-confidence. You are doing good for others and the community, which provides a natural sense of accomplishment. Your role as a volunteer can also give you a sense of pride and identity. And the better you feel about yourself, the more likely you are to have a positive view of your life and future goals.

Volunteering provides a sense of purpose. Older adults, especially those who have retired or lost a spouse, can find new meaning and direction in their lives by helping others. Whatever your age or life situation, volunteering can help take your mind off your own worries, keep you mentally stimulated, and add more zest to your life.

Volunteering helps you stay physically healthy. Studies have found that those who volunteer have a lower mortality rate than those who do not. Older volunteers tend to walk more, find it easier to cope with everyday tasks, are less likely to develop high blood pressure, and have better thinking skills. Volunteering can also lessen symptoms of chronic pain and reduce the risk of heart disease.

http://www.helpguide.org/articles/work-career/volunteering-and-its-surprising-benefits.htm

15. How do we make our live poorer if we don't develop the habit of daily service?

Helping others kindles happiness, as many studies have demonstrated. When researchers at the London School of Economics examined the relationship between volunteering and measures of happiness in a large group of American adults, they found the more people volunteered, the happier they were, according to a study in Social Science and Medicine. Compared with people who never volunteered, the odds of being "very happy" rose 7% among those who volunteer monthly and 12% for people who volunteer every two to four weeks. Among weekly volunteers, 16% felt very happy—a hike in happiness comparable to having an income of $75,000–$100,000 versus $20,000, say the researchers. http://www.helpguide.org/articles/work-career/volunteering-and-its-surprising-benefits.htm

16. Review: what were the first three habits? Last is the habit of exercise. Same two questions. What benefits come to those who exercise daily?

Want to feel better, have more energy and perhaps even live longer? Look no further than exercise. The health benefits of regular exercise and physical activity are hard to ignore. And the benefits of exercise are yours for the taking, regardless of your age, sex or physical ability. Need more convincing to exercise? Check out these seven ways exercise can improve your life.

No. 1: Exercise controls weight

Exercise can help prevent excess weight gain or help maintain weight loss. When you engage in physical activity, you burn calories. The more intense the activity, the more calories you burn. You don't need to set aside large chunks of time for exercise to reap weight-loss benefits. If you can't do an actual workout, get more active throughout the day in simple ways — by taking the stairs instead of the elevator or revving up your household chores.

No. 2: Exercise combats health conditions and diseases

Worried about heart disease? Hoping to prevent high blood pressure? No matter what your current weight, being active boosts high-density lipoprotein (HDL), or "good," cholesterol and decreases unhealthy triglycerides. This one-two punch keeps your blood flowing smoothly, which decreases your risk of cardiovascular diseases. In fact, regular physical activity can help you prevent or manage a wide range of health problems and concerns, including stroke, metabolic syndrome, type 2 diabetes, depression, certain types of cancer, arthritis and falls.

No. 3: Exercise improves mood

Need an emotional lift? Or need to blow off some steam after a stressful day? A workout at the gym or a brisk 30-minute walk can help. Physical activity stimulates various brain chemicals that may leave you feeling happier and more relaxed. You may also feel better about your appearance and yourself when you exercise regularly, which can boost your confidence and improve your self-esteem.

No. 4: Exercise boosts energy

Winded by grocery shopping or household chores? Regular physical activity can improve your muscle strength and boost your endurance. Exercise and physical activity deliver oxygen and nutrients to your tissues and help your cardiovascular system work more efficiently. And when your heart and lungs work more efficiently, you have more energy to go about your daily chores. http://www.mayoclinic.org/healthy-lifestyle/fitness/in-depth/exercise/art-20048389

17. What price do the couch potatoes pay?

Exercise and Your Bones

Regular, moderate exercise -- particularly weight-bearing exercises like walking, running, jogging, and dancing -- keeps your bones strong. Studies show that resistance (strengthening) exercises also boost bone mass and keep muscles strong.

Exercise and Your Skin

Exercise also boosts circulation and the delivery of nutrients to your skin, helping to detoxify the body by removing toxins (poisons).

As exercise boosts oxygen to the skin, it also helps increase the natural production of collagen, the connective tissue that plumps your skin. Your skin will "glow" after exercise, because of the increase in blood flow.

Exercise and Stress

Regular exercise reduces the amount of stress hormones in the body, resulting in a slower heart rate, relaxed blood vessels, and lower blood pressure. Increased relaxation after exercise shows on your face with reduced muscle tension.

Exercise and Your Mood

Research shows that regular exercise reduces symptoms of moderate depression and enhances psychological fitness. Exercise can even produce changes in certain chemical levels in the body, which can have an effect on the psychological state.

Endorphins are hormones in the brain associated with a happy, positive feeling. A low level of endorphins is associated with depression. During exercise, plasma levels of this substance increase. This may help to ease symptoms of depression. A recent National Health and Nutrition survey found that physically active people were half as likely to be depressed. http://teens.webmd.com/benefits-of-exercise?page=2

18. Put it all together. How would our lives be different—and better—three months from now if we developed these four habits?

With a strong enough why, almost anything is possible.

With a strong enough why, the how will nearly take care of itself.

With a strong enough why, we can break the nastiest habit.

With a strong enough why, we can start almost any habit and make it stick.

When it comes right down to it, we are just not motivated enough. We don't want it enough. It doesn't mean that much to us. We don't have a strong enough why. — Josh Hunt, *Break a Habit; Make a Habit* (2020 Vision, 2013).

19. And how would our lives be worse if we did not develop these four habits?

How do we get a strong why? Let me list three ways:

1. Make a list of all the reasons you want to form a habit or break a habit. Make the list long. Make it emotional. Make it matter.

2. Make a list of all the bad things that will happen if you don't break that nasty habit. Again, the longer the list, the better.

3. Make a list of all the good things that will happen if you do break the nasty habit. Did I mention to make the list long?

We are all influenced by two things: pain and pleasure. Managers know to motivate with both the carrot and the stick. Parents motivate with rewards and punishments. We do well to motivate ourselves the same way—by getting in our head a long list of why we do want to break a nasty habit and what bad things will happen if we don't. — Josh Hunt, *Break a Habit; Make a Habit* (2020 Vision, 2013).

20. What is your biggest take-away from today's discussion?

21. How can we support one another in prayer this week?

4 Habits, Lesson #2
Psalm 1; John 15.7
The Habit of Quiet Time
Good Questions Have Groups Talking
www.joshhunt.com

OPEN

What is your name and what are three things you do to start your day.

DIG

1. **Psalm 1. Imagine you are reading this Psalm in your daily Quiet Time. What verses pop out at you?**

   Psalm 1 has a message of guidance for each person today. It presents a clear distinction between two kinds of people: the righteous and the wicked. The first and last words of this psalm reveal the ultimate destiny of each group. The righteous are "blessed" (v. 1) and the wicked "perish" (v. 6).

   In verses 1-3 you find a description of the righteous person. The righteous person does not seek or follow the advice of those who live a lifestyle which is counter to the Word of God. Nor does he spend time with these people. When a person ignores the guidance of these verses, the impact of associating with the ungodly often seeps into a marriage relationship. It may not be apparent at first, but soon attitudes and eventually behaviors begin to change and a spiritual erosion takes place.

The godly use the Word of God as their guide for life, and they meditate upon it. The heart of meditation is studying and reflecting upon the meaning of Scripture and how it applies to our lives. God's Word is to be our guide for life; we're not to replace it with the opinions of talk show hosts, the Wall Street Journal, trendy self-help books, or the advice of our coworkers in the office.

What are the results of focusing your life and marriage on the Word of God? Like a tree planted by streams of waters, you will be strengthened and refreshed each day. It's a guaranteed benefit available to you!

What about you? Whom do you spend time with and listen to? Talk about how the two main categories in Psalm 1—the righteous and the wicked—influence your life and your marriage. — H. Norman Wright, *Quiet Times for Couples* (Eugene, OR: Harvest House, 2011).

2. What exactly does it mean to meditate?

The phrase "meditate on his law day and night" may sound intimidating, unrealistic, or undesirable. How would I ever get any work done if I spent the whole day contemplating Lamentations? But that's not necessary. That is not the idea.

There is an old saying that if you can worry, you can meditate. Meditating is simply turning a thought over and over in your mind. As you do that, neurons are firing and your brain is rewiring. When you receive information that matters to you, you can't help meditating on it.

When I was in high school, a friend of mine told me about a girl who liked me. I could not believe it, because I knew this girl and she was way out of my league.

"This can't be true," I said.

"But it is true," my friend said. "I don't understand it either, but it's true."

That night my mind fixated on this thought: She likes me. I couldn't stop thinking about it. My mind just went there over and over. She likes me. So the next day, although I could hardly believe it was true, I called her up and asked her out.

It turned out it wasn't true.

But I had one really good night thinking about it. It was my delight, and what I delight in, I can't help thinking about.

What would it look like to delight in the law of the Lord? It certainly is something deeper than being thrilled about a bunch of rules in the Bible. It starts with a vision of being loved by God. God is way out of my league. He is in the perfection league; I am in the fallen league. This wonderful God, this mysterious, all-powerful, all-holy God — he loves me! Periodically this truth bursts in, and we can't stop thinking about it.

He loves me! — John Ortberg, *The Me I Want to Be* (Grand Rapids, MI: Zondervan, 2010).

3. How are Christian meditation and eastern meditation different?

In contrast to Eastern meditation, which seeks to empty the mind, Christian meditation seeks to focus and fill the mind with the truth of God. While Eastern meditation

puts aside reason, Christian meditation develops the skillful use of reason, considering the works of God and seeking to understand what they mean. Christian meditation also includes the emotions. We focus on God and his Word so much that we feel glad about God's truth, humbled by his law, thrilled with his creation. Christian meditation combines reflection with emotion in such a way as to produce poetry such as the psalms.
— Stephen D. Eyre, *Drawing close to God: The Essentials of a Dynamic Quiet Time: A Lifeguide Resource* (Downers Grove, IL: InterVarsity Press, 1995).

4. What good things come to those who meditate?

Years ago I read of the construction of a city hall and fire station in a small Pennsylvania community. The citizens were so proud of their new red brick structure—a long-awaited dream come true. Not too many weeks after moving in, however, strange things began to happen. Several doors failed to shut completely and a few windows wouldn't slide open very easily. As time passed, ominous cracks began to appear in the walls. Within a few months, the front door couldn't be locked . . . and the roof began to leak. By and by, the little building that was once the source of great pride had to be condemned. An intense investigation revealed that deep mining blasts several miles away caused underground shock waves that subsequently weakened the earth beneath the building foundation, resulting in its virtual self-destruction.

So it is with compromise in a life. Slowly, almost imperceptibly, one rationalization leads to another, which triggers a series of equally damaging alterations in a life that was once stable, strong, and reliable. — *Living Beyond the Daily Grind* / Charles R. Swindoll, *Wisdom for* the Way: Wise Words for Busy People (Nashville: Thomas Nelson, 2007).

5. What exactly does it mean to be blessed?

The first word, "blessed," is somewhat bland in our English language. The Hebrew term is much more descriptive, especially with its plural ending. Perhaps a workable rendering would be, "Oh, the happiness, many times over. . . ." — Charles R. Swindoll, *Living the Psalms: Encouragement for the Daily Grind* (Brentwood, TN: Worthy Publishing, 2012).

6. John 15.1 - 7. What do we learn about prayer from this passage?

Mr. Marconi, famous for inventing radio technology, once constructed a receiver that would only respond to a special transmitter. If the transmitter radiated eight hundred thousand vibrations a second the receiver would only take from the same rate of vibration. In the same way, the familiar tuning-fork will only respond to another tuning-fork of precisely the same musical tone. This is the principle of assured answer to prayer. If I am right with God, tuned to his purposes and will, I cannot ask in vain. "If ye abide in me and my words abide in you, ye shall ask what ye will and it shall be done unto you" (John 15:7). God's response to our petitions follows our response to His commands. "Delight thyself also in the Lord and He shall give thee the desires of thine heart" (Ps. 37:4). Affinity of soul with God is assurance of His hearing us. — *AMG Bible Illustrations, Bible Illustrations Series* (Chattanooga: AMG Publishers, 2000).

7. What do we learn about Jesus?

THE VINE

Jesus said, "I am the true vine" (John 15:1).

Okay, you might think of a vine as the long, skinny, winding part of a plant that climbs up your grandma's fence in the summertime. Not so with a grapevine. With grapes, the vine is more like a trunk. It grows out of the ground and supports the rest of the plant. A healthy vine has a root system that goes deep into the soil to draw water into the plant. This water gives the plant life. It becomes sap, which flows through the vine and into the branches. Eventually, it produces juicy grapes. A well-kept vine grows about three or four feet tall. And it's sturdy enough to feed a whole system of branches. The vinedresser usually supplies some sort of support for these branches.

THE VINEDRESSER

Jesus said, "My Father is the vinedresser" (John 15:1).

The vinedresser's task is simple: to take care of the plants and help them produce as many grapes as possible. The better the vinedresser cares for a vineyard, the more grapes it will produce for harvesting at the end of the season. — Bruce Wilkinson, *Secrets of the Vine*™ *for Kids* (Nashville: Thomas Nelson, 2002).

8. What do we learn about ourselves?

Jesus said, "You are the branches" (15:5).

Lots of branches can grow out of each grapevine. Each branch usually grows in a different direction, and each one bears fruit. The branches get fed by the vine, which helps them to grow and climb. And the vinedresser ties these sturdy branches to supports so they don't get too heavy and break. The healthier and stronger the branch, the more grapes it will grow.

THE FRUIT

Jesus said, "You should go and bear fruit" (15:16).

The goal behind all the hard work of tending, pruning, weeding, and watering the grapevines is to get a whole lot of grapes to harvest. In other words—it's all about the fruit. And with the right care, each branch can grow lots of grapes. — Bruce Wilkinson, *Secrets of the Vine*™ *for Kids* (Nashville: Thomas Nelson, 2002).

9. What exactly does it mean to abide in Christ?

The Christian life is neither hard nor difficult; it is actually impossible without abiding in Christ. To abide in Christ means to have a desperate dependence and a restful residence in the Lord. I went with Kelly to a doctor's appointment as the due date for our son was approaching. Watching the sonogram, it was incredible to have a window into where God does His knitting. The sonogram was black and white, and yet suddenly, streaks of color began to pop up on the screen. The doctor pointed out that those colors were nutrients passing through the umbilical cord. Greyson was abiding in Kelly—desperately dependent on her for nourishment and yet resting peacefully. For me, it was a stunning picture of our abiding in the True Vine.

The call on our lives is not to bear fruit but to abide. If we abide, the fruit will take care of itself. Matthew 6:33 reminds us, "Seek first his kingdom and his righteousness, and all these things will be given to you as well." The question is not what we can do for Him but what can He do through us. Abiding dependently and restfully, not on our own efforts, is the route to bearing lasting fruit. The abiding life allows God to live through us. The Holy Spirit moves through believers as they surrender. We still prepare and plan, but we do so knowing that it is not our strength that brings the tipping point. We aren't the source; He is. A yielded and yet prepared heart is the place of strength. — Gregg Matte, *I Am Changes Who I Am: Who Jesus Is Changes Who I Am, What Jesus Does Changes What I Am to Do* (Grand Rapids, MI: Baker, 2012).

10. We always want to read the Bible for application. What is the application of this passage? There can be several right answers.

Your father wants to answer prayer. If you are abiding in Christ, and if his Word abides in you, then you will pray in his will and he will answer. "And this is the confidence which we have before Him, that if we ask anything according to His will, He hears us" (1 John 5:14). It has well been said that prayer is not getting man's will done in heaven, but getting God's will done on earth. It is not overcoming God's reluctance but laying hold of God's willingness.

What a joy it is to have God answer prayer! What confidence it gives you to know that you can take "everything to God in prayer" and he will hear and answer! He does not always give us what we ask, but he does give us what we need, when we need it. This is one of the evidences of abiding. —WARREN W. WIERSBE / Thomas Nelson, *A Daybook of Prayer: Meditations, Scriptures and Prayers to Draw near to the Heart of God* (Nashville: Thomas Nelson, 2007).

11. Do you think God is ever irritated that our prayers are too big? Do you think we pray for too much?

How "large" should Christians dare to pray? According to the witness of the Gospels, as large as our minds can conceive, so long as we are in Christ and praying according to His will.

Jesus regularly admonished His disciples to pray for anything in His name. In the Sermon on the Mount, Jesus said, "Ask, and it will be given" (Matthew 7:7). The same words appear a second time, in a different setting, in Luke's gospel (Luke 11:9). Both Matthew and Mark give us the message of Jesus' saying, "Whatever you ask in prayer, you will receive, if you have faith" (Matthew 21:22; see also Mark 11:24). John's gospel records several instances of Jesus' having spoken these and similar words, including the statement, "If you abide in me, and my words abide in you, ask whatever you wish, and it will be done for you" (John 15:7). — The Navigators, *Dawson Trotman: In His Own Words* (Colorado Springs, CO: NavPress, 2014).

12. **If we are going to live lives abiding in Christ, we do well to starting our day focusing our thoughts on Him. We do well to starting our day meditating on God's Word. This is what we mean by a Quiet Time. Imagine I am a new believer. How would you explain to me about what a Quiet Time is, and why it is important?**

Bob Magnuson was one of my first spiritual mentors. He and his wife, Judy, had discovered the secret to a powerful, effective ministry to young college men: food. Every Thursday evening I joined them for the best spaghetti and cinnamon rolls on the planet. But it was the feast after dinner that filled my real hunger.

Each week, Bob and I would read and discuss the Bible. Bob's favorite quote from Jesus was from Jn. 6:63: "The words I have spoken to you are spirit and they are life." The Scriptures always came alive when Bob talked about them.

Bob helped me begin to develop my own relationship with God. He understood that the substance of Jesus' ministry to His disciples was to pass on to them His relationship with His heavenly Father. In the same way, Bob brought me into God's presence. He let me in on the intimacy he had with his Savior, and I began to learn what it meant to know and love God. Bob modeled what it looked like to relate closely to God and taught me how to sustain that relationship through a daily quiet time.

Helping another person become more intimate with God is an essential goal of discipleship. Teaching that person how to have a quiet time on his own is one practical way to accomplish this goal. What follows is a simple guide to that process. — *Discipleship Journal, Issue 116* (March/ April 2000) (NavPress, 2000).

13. A popular business book has the title, *Start with Why*. Let's start with why. Why should we have a Quiet Time? What is the purpose of a Quiet Time?

The purpose of spending time alone with God daily is to develop intimacy with Him and to learn how He wants us to live. When I begin to teach someone about a personal quiet time, I believe it's important to help him see the biblical basis for this practice. To accomplish that, I ask him to consider what the following passages say about the value of spending time with God regularly.

Ex. 33:11	Ps. 16:11
Ps. 73:25–28	Jer. 2:32
Mt. 11:28–30	Lk. 10:38–42
Ps. 5:1–3	Ps. 27:4
Ps. 143:8	Mt. 4:4
Mk. 1:35	Heb. 4:14–15

After he's had a week or two to take a look at these scriptures, we discuss the following questions:

- What is a quiet time?

- How often would it be good for me to spend time alone with God?

- When during the day did people spend time with God?

- What might be my purpose when I have a quiet time?

- What is God's desire when I meet with Him?

- What might I hope to gain by having quiet times regularly?

This exercise helps establish the conviction that having a quiet time daily is a practice God's Word describes and endorses. — *Discipleship Journal, Issue 116* (March/April 2000) (NavPress, 2000).

14. How long does a Quiet Time take?

Most Christians will tell you that they firmly believe in the importance of spending regular time in God's Word and in prayer each day. Yet, so many of us struggle to do this consistently. Perhaps that's because we think this time with God has to be a monumental, mystical experience. In fact, you can begin developing this spiritual discipline in as little as seven minutes a day.

Longtime Navigator Bob Foster developed a simple outline, called Seven Minutes with God, to help deepen your daily relationship with the Father.

"This is simply a guide," Bob emphasized. "Very soon you will discover that it is impossible to spend only seven minutes with the Lord. An amazing thing happens—seven minutes become 20, and it's not long before you're spending 30 precious minutes with Him."

Do It for the Right Reason

Bob also offered additional words of wisdom: "Do not become devoted to the habit, but to the Savior. Do it not because other [people] are doing it—not as a spiritless duty every morning, not merely as an end in itself, but because God has granted the priceless privilege of fellowship with Himself."

Want a deeper walk with God? Give Him just seven minutes and see what happens!

You may order copies of the booklet Seven Minutes with God from NavPress.

½ Minute: Preparing Your Heart

Invest the first 30 seconds preparing your heart. You might pray, "Lord, cleanse my heart so You can speak to me through the Scriptures. Make my mind alert, my soul active, and my heart responsive. Surround me with Your presence during this time."

4 Minutes: Listening to God (Scripture Reading)

Take the next four minutes to read the Bible. Your greatest need is to hear a word from God. Allow the Word to strike fire in your heart. Meet the Author!

2½ Minutes: Talking to God (Prayer)

After God has spoken through His Book, then speak to Him in prayer. One method is to incorporate four areas of prayer that you can remember with the word ACTS.

Adoration. This is the purest kind of prayer because it's all for God. Tell the Lord that you love Him. Reflect on His greatness.

Confession. Having seen Him, you now want to be sure every sin is cleansed and forsaken. "Confession" comes from a root word meaning "to agree together with." When we apply this to prayer, it means we agree with God's estimation of what we've done.

Thanksgiving. Think of several specific things to thank Him for: your family, your business, your church—even thank Him for hardships.

Supplication. This means to "ask for, earnestly and humbly." Ask for others, then ask for yourself. Include people around the world, missionaries, friends, and those who have yet to hear about Jesus.

15. What exactly do you do during a Quiet Time?

After we've established the biblical basis for quiet time, I like to show him how to do it. So we have a quiet time together.

Psalms is an excellent book to help a young believer begin to relate intimately and personally to God. I usually select a psalm that corresponds to the day of the month or one that is related to an issue the person is facing. We read the entire psalm together and then go back and alternate reading one or two verses at a time. As we do so, we respond to God by praying those verses back to Him. The intent is to interact with what God is saying in the verse in a way that connects it to our lives.

For example, if I read "The Lord is my shepherd, I shall not be in want" (Ps. 23:1), I might pray, "Lord, thank You for taking care of my needs." Because I am almost always anxious about something, I mention that specific concern in my prayer and state my trust in God to take care of it. Make sure to pray about the things that are important and personal to you, just as you would if you were having a quiet time alone with God. Then let your friend have a turn, and pay attention to what he prays.

Using Psalms in this way creates plenty of opportunities for vulnerability before God about the issues of day-to-day life. I have to be prepared to confess sin, to acknowledge my weaknesses, and to throw myself on God's grace and mercy. — *Discipleship Journal, Issue 116* (March/April 2000) (NavPress, 2000).

16. A lot of us have heard about the importance of having a Quiet Time. We have heard about the importance of having a Quiet Time. But, having a Quiet Time has not become a habit. How can we turn intention into habit?

If you are a church leader—perhaps you are a pastor, or you lead a small group—you would do well to concentrate on this point. Leading people to live Christianly comes down to this: leading people into the habit of a Christian Quiet Time.

I can summarize Christian living as one habit: the habit of the Quiet Time. There is much that will come after this—service and evangelism and all kinds of character development. But, it all flows out of the time alone with God in prayer and in His Word.

If we can get people to get the Quiet Time right, there is a good chance that all else will follow. If we don't get the

Quiet Time right, we might do more harm than good. What do I mean by that?

There is always a danger of inoculating people against the gospel rather than infecting them with it. We give them a small dose of the gospel and they think they have the real disease. Thus, they are not interested in true Christianity because they think they have experienced true Christianity.

But, what they have experienced is a country mile from true Christianity. It is churchianity. It is bootstrapianity. It is the stuff of the Pharisees—the stuff that Jesus railed mercilessly against.

There is no Christian living without the Quiet Time. There is no Christian living without prayer. There is no Christian living without being transformed by the renewing of our mind. (Romans 12:2) This is done through time in the Word.

If you are a pastor, you can boil your job down to this: get people into the habit of a Quiet Time. If you are a small group leader, you can distill your job to this: help people form the habit of a Quiet Time. Once you do that, discipleship will follow as surely as night follows day. Simple, right? — Josh Hunt, *The Habit of Discipleship* (Pulpit Press, 2015).

17. How hard is it to move from intention to habit as it relates to Quiet Time?

Good habits: hard to form, easy to live with

There is a difference between simple and easy. It is simple to get from my house in New Mexico to Jacksonville, FL. Just hop on I-10, which runs through the south side of Las Cruces, where I live. Head east on I-10 for two days, eight hours, and fourteen minutes. Stick your toe in the Atlantic surf. Simple, but not easy.

Making disciples is simple: lead people into the habit of a daily Quiet Time. Simple, but not easy.

How hard is it to form a habit and make it stick? The medical community provides some insight into the incredible difficulty of making a habit stick.

Dr. Edward Miller is dean of the medical school and chief executive officer of the hospital at John Hopkins University. He gave a speech at Rockefeller University, an elite medical research center in New York City.

He talked about patients whose arteries are so clogged that any kind of exertion is terribly painful for them. It hurts too much to take a long walk. It hurts too much to make love. So surgeons have to implant pieces of plastic to prop open their arteries, or remove veins from their legs to stitch near the heart so the blood can bypass the blocked passages. The procedures are traumatic and expensive— they can cost more than $100,000. More than one and a half million people every year in the United States undergo coronary bypass graft or angioplasty surgery at a total price of around $60 billion. Although these surgeries are astonishing feats, they are no more than temporary fixes. The operations relieve the patients' pain, at least for a while, but only rarely—fewer than 3 percent of the cases— prevent the heart attacks they're heading toward or prolong their lives. The bypass grafts often clog up within a few years; the angioplasties, in only a few months.

Knowing these grim statistics, doctors tell their patients: If you want to keep the pain from coming back, and if you don't want to have to repeat the surgery, and if you want to stop the course of your heart disease before it kills you, then you have to switch to a healthier lifestyle. You have to stop smoking, stop drinking, stop overeating, start exercising, and relieve your stress.

But very few do.

"If you look at people after coronary-artery bypass grafting two years later, ninety percent of them have not changed their lifestyle," Miller said. "And that's been studied over and over and over again. And so we're missing some link in there. Even though they know they have a very bad disease and they know they should change their lifestyle, for whatever reason, they can't."

"For whatever reason…" What reason? Bad habits— even life threatening bad habits—are extremely hard to break. Good habits are extremely hard to form. "Good habits are hard to form and easy to live with. Bad habits are easy to form and hard to live with. If we don't consciously form good ones, we will unconsciously form bad ones."

Making disciples is simple: get people to have a Quiet Time. But, never confuse this with easy. — Josh Hunt, *The Habit of Discipleship* (Pulpit Press, 2015).

18. **Last week we talked about a two step process to forming a habit. The first one was, "set a low bar." What did we mean by that? How does it relate to Quiet Time? Do you recall the second step?**

The key to developing almost any habit comes down to this:

- Set a low bar

- Go for ruthless consistency

Set a low bar—don't try to read through the Bible in a year at first. Get the Book open every day. There is a verse in Nehemiah that says that, "Ezra opened the book..." This is the key to life-changing Bible study. Open the Book. Open it every day. You don't have to read a lot. You do have to do it every day. Go for ruthless consistency. Don't allow any exceptions. Get the Book open every single day. — Josh Hunt, *The Habit of Discipleship* (Pulpit Press, 2015).

19. **Here is my closing challenge for you. I'd like to challenge you to set a goal of having 100 consecutive days starting your day with your Bible on your lap. Set a low bar. Read one chapter. Pray about what you read about. Seven minutes. After 100 days, this life-changing habit will be firmly established. Who will join me in this challenge? Could we grant permission to one another to ask about this in coming weeks?**

Whether you are involved in a task, recovery, or growth group, making yourself accountable to another member or to the whole group can benefit you. Christian accountability will increase your sensitivity to God's will and His call to obedience. — *Discipleship Journal, Issue 74* (March/April 1993) (NavPress, 1993).

20. How can we support one another in prayer this week?

4 Habits, Lesson #3
Psalm 100 / The Habit of Gratitude
Good Questions Have Groups Talking
www.joshhunt.com

Email your group and invite them to do a little reading on the benefits of gratitude. There has been lots of scientific research on this.

OPEN
What is your name and three things you are grateful for.

DIG
1. **Last week we talked about starting our day with our Bible on our lap. We set a goal of 100 consecutive days spending at least seven minutes with God. How did it go this week? What did you read? What are you praying about? What did it mean to you? How did God speak to you?**

   Generally speaking, accountability is a willingness to share our activities, conduct, and fulfillment of assigned responsibilities with others.

   Accountability is not a new concept. Each of us is accountable in many ways to different organizations and people. If you have a job, you are accountable to your employer, who expects certain things of you. If you don't fulfill your responsibility, the employer has every right to ask you why. If you are married, you are accountable.

Your spouse and family expect certain things. If you are not faithful to your responsibilities, more than likely they will voice their disappointment or concern.

But when it comes to our character and spiritual development, we are prone to resist accountability. "After all," we reason, "that's between me and God. It's nobody else's business."

Many believers mistakenly believe that the personal nature of our relationship with God excludes our need for mutual accountability. Although it is true that our relationship with God is personal in nature, it is not true that it is private. The Bible teaches that we are accountable to one another for our conduct and character.

Specifically, what we are talking about is inviting a person or small group of people to monitor you in one or more areas of your life. For instance, it could be as simple as asking your spouse to check with you from time to time about the consistency of your quiet time. You may want to ask a friend to check with you periodically on how much time you are devoting to your family. I know several men who have accountability partners to keep a check on their choice of entertainment when they are traveling alone. — Charles Stanley, *Handbook for Christian Living* (Nashville: Thomas Nelson, 2008).

2. **With a strong enough "why" almost anything is possible. Why do you want to develop the habit of Quiet Time?**

No Spiritual Discipline is more important than the intake of God's Word. Nothing can substitute for it. There simply is no healthy Christian life apart from a diet of the milk and meat of Scripture. The reasons for this are obvious. In the Bible God tells us about Himself, and especially about Jesus Christ, the incarnation of God. The Bible unfolds the Law of God to us and shows us how we've all broken it. There we learn how Christ died as a sinless, willing Substitute for breakers of God's Law and how we must repent and believe in Him to be right with God. In the Bible we learn the ways and will of the Lord. We find in Scripture how to live in a way that is pleasing to God as well as best and most fulfilling for ourselves. None of this eternally essential information can be found anywhere else except the Bible. Therefore if we would know God and be Godly, we must know the Word of God—intimately. — Donald S. Whitney, *Spiritual Disciplines for the Christian Life* (Colorado Springs, CO: NavPress, 1991), 28.

3. Psalm 100. What do we learn about drawing close to God from this Psalm?

God's command to be thankful is not the threatening demand of a tyrant. Rather, it is the invitation of a lifetime–the opportunity to draw near to Him at any moment of the day.

Do you sometimes long for a greater sense of God's nearness? When pressures intensify, when nighttime worries magnify in strength, when the days are simply piling up one after another, or when life simply feels dull and routine, do you crave the assurance of His presence?

The Scripture says that God inhabits the praises of His people (see Psalm 22:3 KJV). God lives in the place of praise. If we want to be where He is, we need to go to His address.

This is a recurring theme in the psalms: "Enter his gates with thanksgiving, and his courts with praise!"

(Psalm 100:4). "Let us come into his presence with thanksgiving" (95:2). Thanks-giving ushers us into the very presence of God! — Nancy Leigh DeMoss and Lawrence Kimbrough, *Choosing Gratitude: Your Journey to Joy* (Chicago, IL: Moody Publishers, 2009).

4. **As we read the Word, we always do well to read with an ear for emotion. What is the emotion of this Psalm?**

    People who love and have a true relationship with Jesus experience newfound freedom from sin, which gives them a fresh revelation of His truth that can't do anything but make them excited about worshiping Him!

    When you have that type of experience, you become contagious—your enthusiasm infects everyone around you! It seems like the Church today is more concerned with wealth, health and happiness, as if comfort and luxury are the measuring stick for a successful life.

    Why is there such a lukewarm spirit when it comes to being enthusiastic about God? It seems like the announcement of a Super Bowl party after church service gets a more enthusiastic response than a pastor who has to pull teeth to get people to stand up and lift their hands before Jesus in praise. — Lauren Barlow, *Inspired by Tozer: 59 Artists, Writers and Leaders Share the Insight and Passion They've Gained from A.W. Tozer* (Grand Rapids, MI: Baker, 2011).

5. **We want to read for emotion. We also want to read for application. What is the application of this Psalm?**

    The worship we give to the Lord and the work we do for Him must always be done with gladness. When I look around, I realize the men I most respect are men who serve the Lord. When I look ahead, I realize that anything I do—even if it's nothing more than offering a cup of cold water in the Lord's name—will be rewarded (Matthew 10:42). When I look back, I realize the enemy attacks the people at the back of the pack—those who aren't serving the Lord (Deuteronomy 25:18). Therefore, the best place to be is in the front lines, serving the Lord wholeheartedly. — Jon Courson, *Jon Courson's Application Commentary: Volume Two: Psalms-Malachi* (Nashville, TN: Thomas Nelson, 2006), 122–123.

6. Why is it important that we worship the Lord gladly?

People are uncomfortable saying that we are duty-bound to pursue joy.

They say things like, "Don't pursue joy; pursue obedience." But Christian Hedonism responds, "That's like saying, 'Don't eat apples; eat fruit.'" Because joy is an act of obedience. We are commanded to rejoice in God. If obedience is doing what God commands, then joy is not merely the spin-off of obedience, it is obedience. The Bible tells us over and over to pursue joy: "Be glad in the LORD and rejoice, you righteous ones; and shout for joy, all you who are upright in heart" (Psalm 32:11). "Let the nations be glad and sing for joy" (Psalm 67:4). "Delight yourself in the LORD" (Psalm 37:4). "Rejoice that your names are recorded in heaven" (Luke 10:20). "Rejoice in the Lord always; again I will say, rejoice!" (Philippians 4:4).

The Bible does not teach that we should treat delight as a mere by-product of duty. C. S. Lewis got it right when he wrote to a friend, "It is a Christian duty, as you know, for everyone to be as happy as he can." Yes, that is risky and controversial. But it is strictly true. Maximum happiness, both qualitatively and quantitatively, is precisely what we are duty-bound to pursue.

One wise Christian described the relationship between duty and delight this way:

> Suppose a husband asks his wife if he must kiss her good night. Her answer is, "You must, but not that kind of a must." What she means is this: "Unless a spontaneous affection for my person motivates you, your overtures are stripped of all moral value."

In other words, if there is no pleasure in the kiss, the duty of kissing has not been done. Delight in her person, expressed in the kiss, is part of the duty, not a by-product of it. — John Piper, *The Dangerous Duty of Delight* (Sisters, OR: Multnomah Publishers, 2001), 13–14.

7. What if I don't feel glad? What to do then?

It is true that our hearts are often sluggish. We do not feel the depth or intensity of affections appropriate for God or His cause. It is true that at those times we must, insofar as it lies within us, exert our wills and make decisions that we hope will rekindle our joy. Though joyless love is not our aim ("God loves a cheerful giver!"), nevertheless it is better to do a joyless duty than not to do it, provided there is a spirit of repentance for the deadness of our hearts.

I am often asked what a Christian should do if the cheerfulness of obedience is not there. It is a good question. My answer is not to simply get on with your duty because feelings are irrelevant! My answer has three steps. First, confess the sin of joylessness. Acknowledge the culpable coldness of your heart. Don't say that it doesn't matter how you feel. Second, pray earnestly that God would restore the joy of obedience. Third, go ahead and do the outward dimension of your duty in the hope that the doing will rekindle the delight. (For more practical counsel on fighting for joy, see appendix 4.)

This is very different from saying, "Do your duty because feelings don't count." These steps are predicated on the assumption that there is such a thing as hypocrisy. They are based on the belief that our goal is the reunion of pleasure and duty and that a justification of their separation is a justification of sin. — John Piper, *Desiring God* (Sisters, OR: Multnomah Publishers, 2003), 300–301.

8. What do the gates and courts refer to in verse 4?

Notice the imagery of verse 4. The psalmist is writing against the backdrop of the temple worship of the Old Testament. He's telling the people of His day to come to Jerusalem, to the temple. Enter its gates with a thankful spirit and come into the temple courts with praise.

Most of us don't live in Jerusalem, and the Jewish temple is no longer standing; but we can do exactly as the writer says whenever we pray, whenever we praise God in private, and whenever we attend corporate worship services at church or elsewhere. — Robert J. Morgan, *100 Bible Verses Everyone Should Know by Heart* (Nashville: B&H, 2010).

9. Is gratitude an attitude or an activity? Is it an emotion or something we do?

Nothing predicts joy like gratitude. The fastest, most predictable path to joy is gratitude. If you will get in the habit of doing what Paul says he does you will be well on our way to experiencing pure joy.

Gratitude is something you do. It is a behavior. It is action. It is not just an attitude you possesses. It is an activity you perform.

Write a letter to someone you are grateful for. Don't just think happy thoughts. Write a letter. Go to their house. Don't just feel gratitude. Drive. Read. Hug. Cry. Science predicts you will be happier and the effect will last.

Science loves experiments where we have one randomly selected group is assigned one task while the other half is assigned another. If we assign one group the ice cream diet and the other group the meat and vegetables diet we can be sure that it is the diet that caused the difference. The random selection insures that it is the diet and not something else that is making the difference. This is why Martin Seligman was so excited to report this study:

> Robert Emmons and Mike McCullough randomly assigned people to keep a daily diary for two weeks, either of happenings they were grateful for, of hassles, or simply of life events. Joy, happiness, and life satisfaction shot up for the gratitude group.

Science and the Bible agree: gratitude predicts joy. — Josh Hunt, *Pure Joy*, 2013.

10. We discussed this on week one, but it bears repeating. What good things come to the grateful?

Here are five more ways gratitude can positively impact people's lives, based on specific studies:

1. Grateful people are more hopeful and healthier

Like many other studies, this 2015 paper in the Journal of Religion and Health found that those who were more grateful for who they are and what they have were more hopeful and also physically healthier. Psychology Today cites several studies that found people who report being more grateful also report feeling fewer aches and pains, and are more likely to go to the doctor and take care of themselves.

Some of this can possibly be shrugged off as a by-product of happiness: Those who are feeling better tend to be more thankful. But this is not always the case. Dozens of studies have shown that when people actively take the time to list the things they are grateful for, they feel better mentally and physically than participants who haven't done the same.

In other words, gratitude's benefits are not only correlational, but in some cases causal. Gratitude can act "directly, as a causal agent of well-being; and indirectly, as a means of buffering against negative states and emotions," reads a 2009 paper in Counselling Psychology Review.

2. Improved sleep quality

Something as simple as writing down a list of things you are thankful for at the end of the day can also help people sleep better. A 2009 study in the Journal of Psychosomatic Research found that those who expressed gratitude more often slept better and longer than those who didn't.

3. Increased self-esteem

A 2014 paper in the Journal of Applied Sports Psychology found that athletes who expressed more gratitude toward their coaches and also in general had higher self-esteem two and six months later compared to those who weren't as openly thankful.

4. Increased helpfulness and empathy

One 2006 study in the journal Psychological Science found that those who expressed more gratitude were also more likely to help out others. So "pro-social" behaviors are in turn linked to greater happiness.

Empathy also apparently increases when people are thankful. A 2012 paper in Social Psychology and Personality Science found that higher levels of gratitude were linked to greater empathy and lowered aggression. "Gratitude motivates people to express sensitivity and concern for others," the researchers wrote.

5. Increased resilience

In a 2006 study in the journal Behaviour Research and Therapy, scientists found that Vietnam War veterans with high levels of gratitude were more resilient, and less impacted by post-traumatic stress disorder. Another 2003 paper in the Journal of Personality and Social Psychology found that people with neuromuscular diseases who kept "gratitude journals" reported a greater sense of well-being and more positive moods at the end of the study, compared with those who didn't make such lists. http://www.newsweek.com/5-scientifically-proven-benefits-gratitude-398582

11. What price do the ungrateful pay?

Thanksgiving is, quite literally, a holiday built upon the notion of giving thanks. If at no other time of the year, it's the one day when we come together with loved ones to express gratitude at the dinner table. Before digging into the turkey feast, we honor the time-old tradition of counting our blessings.

But the ritual of saying grace before a meal far predates its modern context. In fact, expressing gratitude before you eat is one of the most universal behaviors, according to Adrian Butash, author of Bless Your Food: Ancient and Contemporary Graces from Around the World. It's also an ancient one.

According to theologist Laurel Schneider, historically — in a time before the pasteurization and refrigeration of food — blessings were a way of "purifying" the food. They were also an expression of gratitude to various gods and a recognition that the food "is not ours to begin with, but loaned to us," Schneider told Spirituality & Health magazine.

People have given thanks for food since Pagan times, Butash tells The Huffington Post. There is evidence of mealtime prayers as far back as 2,500 BC in the ancient Hindu food blessings found in the early Vedic text The Mahabharata, and, even further back, food was a common trope in early Paleolithic art, according to Butash.

"Food is a necessity for life, and centuries ago ... if you were starving and got something to eat, you were mighty thankful," Butash says. "Today, we don't think about it that much, but when you think of food as life and death, then you can see how serious it became in the consciousness of the people."

But as much as food is a necessity, it's also a ritual. "Food is so important individually to each of us — both the sustenance and the symbolic meaning," says Butash.

Today, 44 percent of Americans regularly say grace, while 46 percent report almost never saying it. On Thanksgiving, of course, that percentage is much higher.

Whether every night at the dinner table or just on Turkey Day, the practice of saying grace connects us to the food we eat, the people we share it with and the world that has supported and nurtured us with nourishment.

Here's what you should know about saying grace.

Pairing gratitude with a meal can make it even more powerful.

Often, practicing gratitude isn't an activity that we make time for. Sometimes it can even feel like a chore. But by pairing a brief gratitude exercise with an activity that we enjoy and make time for each day (like eating) can help us to make gratitude a more regular part of our lives.

This is rooted in psychology. The Premack Principle of human behavior suggests that when we pair a less desirable activity (in this case, giving thanks) with a more desirable activity (eating), we'll start to derive more enjoyment out of the less desirable activity and be more likely to perform it again. As writer Matt McMinn notes in an article on the Christian blog The Table, pairing a gratitude exercise with the enjoyable and highly reinforcing activity of eating leads us to associate giving thanks with the pleasure we derive from food.

Of course, we don't want to look at giving thanks as an "undesirable" activity — but a little incentive to practice gratitude doesn't hurt!

Taking time for gratitude, just once a day, makes us happy and healthy.

Giving thanks just once a day — maybe at the dinner table, or maybe before bed — for a couple weeks can improve physical and psychological well-being.

Gratitude's value is intrinsic, but its health benefits are also many. Those who take time to be grateful may enjoy improved sleep, lower stress levels, enhanced overall well-being and even improved heart health.

Practicing gratitude has also been linked with stronger personal relationships, higher self-esteem and greater life satisfaction. http://www.huffingtonpost.com/2014/11/26/benefits-of-saying-grace_n_6200202.html

12. How could we turn gratitude from an intention to a habit?

Rejoicing is not an easy task. It is one of the most difficult things you will ever put your mind to. A good way to start is with the activity of gratitude. There are a million ways you can practice gratitude. One thing I often do is make a list of twenty things I am grateful for before I go to bed each night:

- Five family members I am grateful for

- Five other people I am grateful for

- Five physical things I am grateful for

- Five spiritual things I am grateful for.

Over time, gratitude stats to change your mind. The Bible says we are transformed by the renewing of our mind, not by trying really hard to be good. One way to transform the mind is to practice the activity of gratitude. Paul did. He made it a habit to thank God every time he thought of his friends in Philippi. I wonder what else he was in the habit of thanking God for.

Gratitude paves the way to joy. — Josh Hunt, *Pure Joy*, 2013.

13. Let's go around the room and each one share three things you are grateful for. No repeats.

If you struggle with this, it is a hint that this is not a firmly entrenched habit. It ought to be easy to rattle off twenty things you are grateful for. I often do, breaking down the list into the categories above.

14. What keeps us from gratitude?

Consider that Paul lists ingratitude as a hallmark of the world's last days. Do you recognize the following description of a culture on the verge of collapse? "But know this, that in the last days perilous times will come: For men will be lovers of themselves, lovers of money, boasters, proud, blasphemers, disobedient to parents, unthankful, unholy" (2 Timothy 3:1–2).

I think we can all agree that complaining is a contagion of our times. My friend James MacDonald undertook a study of Internet sites that have been set up just for complainers. One of them is The Complaint Station, which claims to have served five million whiners. Another site seems to understand griping as one of life's greatest joys:

> Complain about anything. The whole world is here to listen. Complain about your neighbor. Complain about the airlines. Complain about trains. Complain about noise. Complain about your mother-in-law. Complain about high prices. About getting ripped off. About potholes. About police. Complain about welfare. Complain about work. Complain about your boss. Complain to us. We'll listen and tell everyone. No exceptions!

There are even Christian complaint sites, believe it or not. You can complain that Bible college is too expensive or that nonbelievers curse too much. You can vent about those pastors and church staff members who really bother you. It's difficult to imagine how any follower of Jesus Christ would believe that complaining was a worthwhile or edifying pursuit.

Would you rather be around people who are hateful or grateful? Consider a recent scholarly study on the results of gratitude. It's a bit more difficult to find Web sites devoted to thankfulness than those given to complaining. Yet this 2003 research concluded that grateful people receive a wide range of benefits simply because of their perspective on life. They sleep better and enjoy better physical health. Their social relationships are enhanced. They have a deeper and rewarding sense of spirituality. "Gratitude not only makes people feel good in the present, but it also increases the likelihood that people will function optimally and feel good in the future." Gratitude is one heaping helping of wellness—something more beneficial than ten thousand vitamins or ten years of workouts at the gym.

Grace should create gratitude. And gratitude simply makes the world a far more positive place. It's not surprising to find that the apostle of grace has a great deal to say about the spirit of gratitude. — David Jeremiah, *Captured by Grace: No One Is beyond the Reach of a Loving God* (Nashville, TN: Thomas Nelson Publishers, 2006), 187–188.

15. What could you use as a trigger, or cue to remind you to be grateful first thing in the morning?

The other day I was bounding up the stairs to get something I'd forgotten when I had this realization: Although getting older, I am still healthy enough to climb stairs with ease—in fact, I enjoy it! Suddenly I felt deep gratitude for my good health.

"Gratitude" is a mental attitude I want to cultivate. So it occurred to me...Why not use every instance of stair-climbing as a cue to evoke and savor that wonderful inner feeling of gratitude?

It worked. As I continued to link "gratitude" with "stair-climbing," I found that the "gratitude attitude" would pop up automatically in other situations, especially those involving physical activity like walking or gardening.

Deliberating setting up a cue—like stair-climbing—to trigger a desired emotional state—like gratitude—I was a new idea for me. True, I had often used cues to trigger a behavioral habit or action, like blocking the stairs with the laundry basket so I couldn't possibly forget to carry it down to the laundry room. This time, though, I began to think about how I could use cues as signals to a more positive mental outlook. I came up with seven great ideas that work for me. Adopt them for yourself or use them to imagine how you could create your own cues for positive mental states.

But first...what IS a cue?

Clues to Cues: First Steps

A cue is a signal that reminds your brain to activate a particular emotion, action, or thought.

Without thinking about it, you probably use cues all the time to activate the mental states you need. For example, if you know you are going to meet up with a manipulative person, you will probably activate a mental state of wariness. Or, if you are about to visit a sick friend, you might naturally feel a caring concern as you enter his home.

But you can also deliberately choose cues to create helpful and happier mental attitudes. To do this, you could identify one positive mental state you would like to cultivate or strengthen.

https://www.psychologytoday.com/blog/changepower/201606/create-calm-and-positive-mindset-these-7-simple-cues

16. How do we stay grateful when life is hard?

Gratitude is the ability to have hope in the midst of seeming hopelessness. Gratitude isn't a drug to escape or ignore the reality of desperate circumstances. Instead, it gives us the courage to confront our problems, offering hope where hope cannot be found.

The Bible teaches us to "give thanks in all circumstances" (1 Thessalonians 5:18). "All circumstances" means all circumstances, including the difficult times. This is incredibly difficult, yet when we give thanks in the midst of our trials and challenges, amazing things can happen.

Gratitude is a life skill and the application of God's wisdom. It is the means of holy living. There is an old saying, "Those who do battle without knowing the tactics will lose." In order to conquer the unwanted battles in our life, we should not neglect the strategies.

When we are in a situation where we see nothing to be thankful for, our perspective on the situation may change if we give thanks. Our attitudes can change, for in our gratitude we convey our trust of God and grow in wisdom.

Gratitude can keep us from being discouraged or overwhelmed by fear in the midst of a depressing situation. Even if the situation feels like a storm, for the sake of our family and neighbors, we need to discipline ourselves to keep calm. — Joshua Choonmin Kang, *Spirituality of Gratitude: The Unexpected Blessings of Thankfulness* (Westmont, IL: InterVarsity Press, 2015).

17. Would you say developing habit of gratitude is really important, sort of important, or not so important?

Spend just a few minutes each day focusing on the good things that happened, the incidents and situations that you'd put in the plus column if you were noting plusses and minuses. You'll be healthier. You'll sleep better and exercise more. You'll feel more optimistic. Take just a moment to note the day's blessings and you'll sense that you have more energy. You will feel more alert and active. Do this for a period of time, and you'll realize you are making progress toward your goals in life. You may even discover you're less of a mess, more organized, less possessive-the clutter that used to collect around you seems to disappear. — *Thank You Power: Making the Science of Gratitude Work for You* by Deborah Norville

18. Why is it important to you personally to develop the habit of gratitude?

The people who focused on gratitude were just flat-out happier. They saw their lives in favorable terms. They reported fewer negative physical symptoms, such as headaches or colds, and they were active in ways that were good for them: they spent almost an hour and a half more per week exercising than the people who focused on their hassles. In addition, those who'd been on the receiving end of someone else's kindness rated higher in joy and happiness than the others. In short, those who focused on what they were grateful for felt a higher level of gratitude. Life just seemed better for them.' — *Thank You Power: Making the Science of Gratitude Work for You* by Deborah Norville

19. **Review. What do you want to remember from today's conversation?**

20. **How can we support one another in prayer this week? Also, as we pray, let's remember to thank God for a number of things we are grateful for.**

4 Habits, Lesson #4
John 13.1 - 17 / The Habit of Service
Good Questions Have Groups Talking
www.joshhunt.com

Email your group and invite them to do a little reading on the benefits of volunteering. There has been lots of scientific research on this.

OPEN

What is your name and three things you are grateful for? If you have been practicing, this should be easier than it was a week ago.

DIG

1. **A couple of weeks ago we talked about starting our day with our Bible on our lap. Many of us set a goal of 100 consecutive days and we agreed we would check in on each other. How is it going. If you have missed some days, try to analyze why you missed those days.**

   Seven More Quiet Time Ideas by Dan S. Baty

   1. Listen to a favorite song. Then discuss the lyrics with the Lord. Since lyrics are often very emotional in content, they can inspire heart-level interaction with the Lord.

2. Listen to a taped sermon. Play a tape of a Sunday message for a spiritual boost during the week. You may even want to take a special weekend retreat alone to listen to a series of messages. Make the time like any other "conference" and include breaks, meal times, and recreation.

3. Keep a joy box. Based on the principle that every good thing we experience comes from the Lord (Jas. 1:17), use a box to collect things that have brought you joy: a photo of someone special, a ticket stub from a special event, a souvenir from a special friend. Take this box out every few months and go through it, thanking the Lord for the experiences and relationships.

4. Meet the Lord with someone else—your spouse, a roommate, or a coworker. The Lord promises His presence in a special way where two or three are gathered in His name (Mt. 18:20).

5. Discuss the news. When you have a strong reaction to an article from the newspaper, clip it and save it to discuss with the Lord. This can serve as a good tool to pray for your community and government (1 Tim. 2:2).

6. Record important moments. During the day, make a quick list of happy incidents, bothersome matters, anxious moments, significant comments, etc., and save them for a time when you can discuss them with God.

7. Take a hallelujah hike. Observe creation and praise the Lord for His creativity and splendor. Author Ronald B. Allen wrote, "Wherever we may look in the world that He has made, we may declare with profound awe: Here is where He has been. The whorls of divine prints are conspicuous throughout His creation. — *Discipleship Journal, Issue 74* (March/April 1993) (NavPress, 1993).

2. **There may be someone who was not here the week we talked about Quiet Time. Refresh our memories. What is a Quiet Time and why is it important?**

All that has been said thus far about the importance of prayer, of meditating on the Word of God, and of having a specific time of worship, implies the value of a quiet time. The expression "quiet time" is used to describe a regular period each day set aside to meet with God through His Word and through prayer. One of the great privileges of a believer is to have fellowship with almighty God. We do this by listening to Him speak to us from His Word and by speaking to Him through prayer.

There are various spiritual exercises we may want to accomplish during our quiet time, such as reading through the Bible in a year and praying over certain requests. But the primary objective of our quiet time should be fellowship with God—developing a personal relationship with Him and growing in our devotion to Him.

After I have begun my quiet time with a period of worship, I next turn to the Bible. As I read a passage of Scripture (usually one or more chapters), I talk to God about what I am reading. I like to think of the quiet time as a conversation: God speaking to me through the Bible and I responding to what He says. This approach helps to make the quiet time what it is intended to be—a time of fellowship with God. — Jerry Bridges, *The Fruitful Life: The Overflow of God's Love Through You* (Colorado Springs, CO: NavPress, 2006), 174.

3. **John 13.1 – 17. Let's read this passage out loud. Read for application. What is the main application of this passage?**

   Now that I, your Lord and Teacher, have washed your feet, you also should wash one another's feet. John 13:14 (NIV2011)

4. **Jesus set an example for us by serving. That is one application. I want to illustrate that as we read Scripture, there are often multiple applications. What other application can you find from this story. There can be several right answers.**

   To place our feet in the basin of Jesus is to place the filthiest parts of our lives into his hands. In the ancient East, people's feet were caked with mud and dirt. The servant of the feast saw to it that the feet were cleaned. Jesus is assuming the role of the servant. He will wash the grimiest part of your life.

   If you let him. The water of the Servant comes only when we confess that we are dirty. Only when we confess that we are caked with filth, that we have walked forbidden trails and followed the wrong paths....

   We will never be cleansed until we confess we are dirty. We will never be pure until we admit we are filthy. And we will never be able to wash the feet of those who have hurt us until we allow Jesus, the one we have hurt, to wash ours. — *A Gentle Thunder* / Max Lucado and Terri A. Gibbs, *Grace for the Moment: Inspirational Thoughts for Each Day of the Year* (Nashville, TN: J. Countryman, 2000), 23.

5. **Read for emotion. How do you imagine the disciples felt as Jesus took the towel and the basin of water?**

It's a rather astonishing story all around, but to me, the most amazing fact is that only Peter objected. Didn't it bother the rest that their leader became their servant? — Lauren Barlow, *Inspired by Tozer: 59 Artists, Writers and Leaders Share the Insight and Passion They've Gained from A.W. Tozer* (Grand Rapids, MI: Baker, 2011).

6. **How do you imagine Jesus felt?**

There is no way to remove the jab and the twist from Christ's words to Peter. He said, in effect, "If you do not allow Me to do this, that is it. Get out!" Anybody who lives under the delusion that Christ was rather weak and spineless has overlooked such statements as this one. Being a servant in no way implies there will never be a confrontation or strong words shared with others. The Lord may choose to use the reproof of a servant who has earned the right to be heard even more often than that of an aggressive leader type.

It certainly worked with Peter. We know he got the message when he blurted out, in so many words, "Give me a bath!" No, that wasn't necessary, only his feet. — Charles R. Swindoll, *Improving Your Serve* (Nashville: Thomas Nelson, 2004).

7. **Two other questions we can ask of this text. We can ask these profitably of nearly any text: What we learn about God? (Or, in this case, what do we learn about Jesus?)**

Jesus came to serve and to give. It makes sense, then, to say that God desires the same for us.] After bringing us into His family through faith in His Son, the Lord God sets His sights on building into us the same quality that made Jesus distinct from all others in His day. He is engaged in building into His people the same serving and giving qualities that characterized His Son.

The Son of Man did not come to be served, but to serve. MARK 10:45 — Charles R. Swindoll, *Bedside Blessings* (Nashville: Thomas Nelson, 2006).

8. What do we learn about ourselves?

Jesus looked at this motley crew of ragtag renegades and loved them to the end, or, literally "unto the uttermost." In other words, He loved them with no limit—even though He was aware of their past faltering.

> "Let's call down fire from heaven and kill everyone who doesn't respond to You," said James and John heatedly (see Luke 9:54).

> "Can any good thing come out of Nazareth?" scoffed Nathanael skeptically (see John 1:46).

He was also aware of their future failings.

> "Satan desires to sift you like wheat, Peter," He would say. "But I have prayed for you, and when you come through, strengthen the brothers" (see Luke 22:31, 32).

He was also aware of their present flaws.

> As they sat together in the Upper Room, Luke tells us the disciples were not sitting in ladder-backed chairs gazing piously at Jesus. No, they were reclined around a low table, arguing among themselves about who was the greatest (Luke 22:24).

> Not only was there arguing around the table, but stinking feet underneath the table. You see, it was

customary for a servant to wash the dust off the feet of anyone who entered the home of his master. In this case, however, no one humbled himself to wash feet, so everyone's feet remained dirty.

Past faltering, present failure, future flaws, and stinking feet notwithstanding, Jesus saw His disciples not only in their present vulnerabilities but also in their eventual victory—and loved them to the uttermost. — Jon Courson, *Jon Courson's Application Commentary* (Nashville, TN: Thomas Nelson, 2003), 546.

9. **Background. What do you know about foot-washing back in the day? Perhaps you have study Bible with a note.**

It seems strange that the feet-washing did not precede supper; but Jesus may well have postponed the act to make it more impressive. A host was expected to provide water to wash his guests' feet heated with the dust of the road (Lk. 7:44). When Jesus and his companions were fending for themselves the office would be performed by one of the disciples. But according to Lk. 22:21–30 (where the announcement of the betrayal immediately precedes the quarrel about precedence in the kingdom and Jesus' rejoinder about the nobility of service), the disciples were at the moment standing on their dignity, and none would be willing to stoop to the menial office. So Jesus does it himself; he will 'set them an example'; the washing of one another's feet, like the breaking of bread in the Synoptics, the place of which it here takes, is to be the memorial tribute of the disciples to one who gave himself in service to them (14; Mk. 10:45). The 'laying aside' of his robe is symbolic of the 'laying down' of his life (10:17–18; the Greek word is the same). Common folk wore a tunic and over it a cloak, and the latter,

sometimes even the former, would be removed for work. Jesus thus waited upon his disciples in the garb of a slave. What a contrast to the Emperor Caligula who, Suetonius tells us, required his senators to attend him at table 'succinctos linteo,' like waiters! Note that by making the idea of 'washing,' which cannot but be symbolical of Baptism, the central feature of the incident which for John takes the place of the institution of the Lord's Supper, the Evangelist emphasizes, as in 19:34, the intimate connexion between the two sacraments.
— G. H. C. MacGregor, *The Gospel of John, ed. James Moffatt, The Moffatt New Testament Commentary* (New York: Doubleday, Doran & Company, Inc., 1929), 274–275.

10. Most of us know about Christian service. How do we turn knowledge about service into a habit?

My appeal is to find one or two or three small acts of service you can perform nearly every day. I noticed that from time to time my wife would comment that her Kindle was not charged. So, a few months back I started the habit of plugging in her Kindle for her in the morning. The key is not to paint the town. The key is to find something small that you can do every day that will remind you that you are a servant. Get your spouse a cup of coffee. Take out the trash. Do something— anything—that will get you thinking about and doing for others.

11. Let's brainstorm. Let's make a list—a long list—of small acts of service we could do. At this point, we are not committing to doing anything. We are just brainstorming ideas.

Is serving really a big deal? According to Jesus, it is.

In Mark 10:45, Jesus said "For even the Son of Man did not come to be served, but to serve, and to give his life as a ransom for many." Jesus showed us through His actions that serving others is important.

When we truly understand what Jesus has done for us, we desperately want others to know Him and to find the same joy and hope we have. Telling people is not enough. We have to show them. In James 2:18, Jesus' own brother wrote "Show me your faith without deeds, and I will show you my faith by what I do." The way we serve people shows them who Jesus is.

10 practical ways we can serve someone today:

1. Help your family. (Romans 12:10)

When was the last time you cleaned the dishes or made dinner, not because it was your turn, but just because you can? It's easy to forget that the ones we need to serve the most are often the ones closest to you. How would the attitudes in our homes change if we started each day by asking, "How can I help you today?" then followed through on the response.

2. Volunteer at church. (Peter 4:10-11)

The people who greet you on the way into service, the folks who create copies for KidSpring, writers like me — we're not superhuman. God isn't looking for super-Christians; He's building the church with normal people just like you.

We all have at least one spiritual gift. What do you enjoy doing? What do others say you're good at? What's your schedule look like? These kind of questions can help you discover the place where God wants you to serve the church. Get started here.

3. Donate items to a homeless shelter. (Matthew 25:46)

We all have more than we need. Get the family together and clean out the house gathering clothes, toys, books and coats to donate.

4. Send someone an encouraging note. (1 Thessalonians 5:11)

Encouragement is a gift we can give that costs us nothing. Pick a friend or family member each week and send an email, text or handwritten note telling that person you are proud of them, that you're praying for them, or that you're here to help.

5. Deliver a meal. (Acts 20:35)

When you make dinner, double that recipe and take it to someone who may need a helping hand. A busy mother, a sick friend, or an elderly neighbor would love a night free from worrying about what's for dinner.

6. Watch someone's kids. (Hebrews 13:16)

Do you know a young family that could use a date night? Call them up and offer to babysit...for free!

7. Help other people shine. (Philippians 2:3)

We want people to acknowledge our accomplishments and our successes, but in Philippians, Paul tells us to consider others better than ourselves. Helping others showcase their gifts and talents is an awesome way to serve someone else.

8. Listen. (James 1:19)

Take time to sit with your kids, a friend, your spouse, or a neighbor and just listen to them. Make a point to put your own agenda aside, and focus on what someone else has to say!

9. Pay it forward. (Proverbs 11:24-25)

While in line at the grocery store, coffee shop, or a fast food place, pay for the person behind you, no strings attached. Your generosity could make someone's day.

10. Anticipate serving. (Galatians 6:9)

One of the best ways to find opportunities to serve is ask God to give them to you. God will definitely answer, so be ready to jump in whenever the Holy Spirit nudges you. https://newspring.cc/articles/10-easy-ways-to-serve-someone-today

12. Two questions we can ask ourselves as we consider any application. First: what good things come to those who serve?

Over the past two decades we have also seen a growing body of research that indicates volunteering provides individual health benefits in addition to social ones. This research, which is presented by CNCS in a report titled "The Health Benefits of Volunteering: A Review of Recent Research," has established a strong relationship between volunteering and health: those who volunteer have lower mortality rates, greater functional ability, and lower rates of depression later in life than those who do not volunteer.

Comparisons of the health benefits of volunteering for different age groups have also shown that older volunteers are the most likely to receive greater benefits from volunteering, whether because they are more likely to face higher incidence of illness or because volunteering provides them with physical and social activity and a sense of purpose at a time when their social roles are changing.

Some of these findings also indicate that volunteers who devote a "considerable" amount of time to volunteer activities (about 100 hours per year) are most likely to exhibit positive health outcomes. http://www. nationalservice.gov/serve-your-community/benefits-volunteering

13. And, let's talk about the opposite: what blessings do we miss out if we don't adopt a servant's heart? How are those who don't serve poorer themselves?

A recent article in the Guardian asked the question "Is it time for doctors to prescribe volunteering?" The answer might be yes! Research conducted by the Harvard School of Public Health indicates that "people who volunteered spent 38 percent fewer nights in the hospital" than non-volunteers, and this Atlantic article cites additional findings that volunteers of all ages enjoy better health, more stamina and lower stress levels. With Habitat, you'll find plenty of those satisfying moments that make volunteering such a spiritual lift. And swinging a hammer or mixing cement is good exercise! http://www.habitat. org/blog/benefits-of-volunteering-280

14. What keeps us from helping more than we do? Why don't more people volunteer? Why don't more serve?

Wanting to test what modern-day seminary students would do if they came face-to-face with their own Good Samaritan situation, some prominent researchers crafted a plan and identified a few dozen unaware seminary students as their guinea pigs. They called the subjects into their office one by one and told each that he or she had just been chosen to give an impromptu talk in the recording studio in the next building over.

Half of the students were given the parable of the Good Samaritan as their topic. The rest were assigned different, random topics. Then they were given one of three senses of urgency: some of the students were told they were already late and that they should hurry over to the recording studio; some were told that they had just enough time to get there; and some were told that that they had a little time to spare before they would have to give their talk.

The researchers hired an actor to play the role of a man in need and planted him in a prominent spot along the sidewalk that each of the students would be taking to get to the recording studio. He was disheveled, slumped over, and looked like he had been the victim of a heart attack or something similar. They wanted to find out which of the students would stop to help the hurting man and which ones would walk right by him.

Here's what they found: being pressed for time had a major impact on whether or not the students stopped and showed concern. Sixty-three percent of those who had been told they had some extra time stopped; 45 percent of those who thought they had just enough time stopped; only 10 percent of the students who thought they were already late stopped. Gender, age, race, and religious denomination made no difference. Neither did their speech topic—the people who had the Good Samaritan parable in mind as they walked by were no more likely to stop if they were in a hurry than those who didn't. — Nelson Searcy and Jennifer Dykes Henson, *The Greatness Principle: Finding Significance and Joy by Serving Others* (Grand Rapids, MI: Baker Books, 2012), 86–87.

15. Think about the list we made a moment ago. Pick out three things you could do on a near-daily basis.

Keep it simple. Go for simple, small, doable things. You can pick up a piece of trash. You can plug in a Kindle. You can pour your wife coffee.

16. How do you feel about doing these things? How do you feel about becoming a servant?

THE ORIGINAL IDEA of becoming a servant seemed either wrong or weird to me. I realize now I rejected it because my concept of a servant was something between an African slave named Kunta Kinte straight out of Roots and one of those nameless migrant workers who, at harvest time, populate the farmlands and orchards across America. Both represented ignorance, objects of mistreatment, a gross absence of human dignity, and the epitome of many of the things Christianity opposes.

The mental image turned me off completely. Washing around in my head was a caricature of a pathetic creature virtually without will or purpose in life . . . bent over, crushed in spirit, lacking self-esteem, soiled, wrinkled, and weary. You know, sort of a human mule who, with a sigh, shuffles and trudges down the long rows of life. Don't ask me why, but that was my perception every time I heard the word servant. Candidly, the idea disgusted me.

And confusion was added to my disgust when I heard people (especially preachers) link the two terms servant and leader. They seemed as opposite as light and dark, a classic example of the proverbial round peg in a square hole. I distinctly remember thinking back then, "Who, me a servant! You gotta be kidding!"

Perhaps that's your initial reaction too. If so, I understand. But you're in for a pleasant surprise. I have great news based on some very helpful information that will—if applied—change your mind and then your life. It excites me when I consider how God is going to use these words in this book to introduce to you (as He did to me) the truth concerning authentic servanthood. How desperately we need to improve our serve! — Charles R. Swindoll, *Improving Your Serve* (Nashville: Thomas Nelson, 2004).

17. This last question takes us beyond the scope of this study, but I'd like for us to hint at it here. In the long run, we want to discover our gifting and focus our service in the area of our gifting. Why is this important?

I recently flew to St. Louis on a commercial airline. The attendant was so grumpy I thought she'd had lemons for breakfast. She made her instructions clear: sit down, buckle up, and shut up! I dared not request anything lest she push the eject button.

Perhaps I caught her on the wrong day, or maybe she caught herself in the wrong career.

Two weeks later I took another flight. This attendant had been imported from heaven. She introduced herself to each passenger, had us greet each other, and then sang a song over the intercom! I had to ask her, "Do you like your work?"

"I love it!" she beamed. "For years I taught elementary school and relished each day. But then they promoted me. I went from a class of kids to an office of papers. Miserable! I resigned, took some months to study myself, found this opportunity, and snagged it. Now I can't wait to come to work!"

Too few people can say what she said. Few people do what she did. One job-placement firm suggests only 1 percent of its clients have made a serious study of their skills.

Don't imitate their mistake. "Don't live carelessly, unthinkingly. Make sure you understand what the Master wants" (Eph. 5:17 MSG). You can do something no one else can do in a fashion no one else can do it. Exploring and extracting your uniqueness excites you, honors God, and expands his kingdom. So "make a careful exploration of who you are and the work you have been given, and then sink yourself into that" (Gal. 6:4 MSG).

Discover and deploy your knacks. — Max Lucado, *Cure for the Common Life: Living in Your Sweet Spot* (Nashville, TN: Thomas Nelson Publishers, 2005), 19–20.

18. How do we discover our gifting?

Look at you. Your uncanny ease with numbers. Your quenchless curiosity about chemistry. Others stare at blueprints and yawn; you read them and drool. "I was made to do this," you say.

Heed that inner music. No one else hears it the way you do.

At this very moment in another section of the church building in which I write, little kids explore their tools. Preschool classrooms may sound like a cacophony to you and me, but God hears a symphony.

A five-year-old sits at a crayon-strewn table. He seldom talks. Classmates have long since set aside their papers, but he ponders his. The colors compel him. He marvels at the gallery of kelly green and navy blue and royal purple. Masterpiece in hand, he'll race to Mom and Dad, eager to show them his kindergarten Picasso.

His sister, however, forgets her drawing. She won't consume the home commute with tales of painted pictures. She'll tell tales of tales. "The teacher told us a new story today!" And the girl will need no prodding to repeat it.

Another boy cares less about the story and the drawings and more about the other kids. He spends the day wearing a "Hey, listen to me!" expression, lingering at the front of the class, testing the patience of the teacher. He relishes attention, evokes reactions. His theme seems to be "Do it this way. Come with me. Let's try this."

Meaningless activities at an insignificant age? Or subtle hints of hidden strengths? I opt for the latter. The quiet boy with the color fascination may someday brighten city walls with murals. His sister may pen a screenplay or teach literature to curious coeds. And the kid who recruits followers today might eventually do the same on behalf of a product, the poor, or even his church.

What about you? Our Maker gives assignments to people, "to each according to each one's unique ability" (Matt. 25:15). As he calls, he equips. Look back over your life. What have you consistently done well? What have you loved to do? Stand at the intersection of your affections and successes and find your uniqueness. — Max Lucado, *Cure for the Common Life: Living in Your Sweet Spot* (Nashville, TN: Thomas Nelson Publishers, 2005), 2–3.

19. What do you want to apply from today's study?

20. How can we support one another in prayer this week?

4 Habits, Lesson #5
1 Timothy 4.7 - 8; 1 Corinthians 6.19 - 20
The Habit of Exercise
Good Questions Have Groups Talking
www.joshhunt.com

Email your group and invite them to do a little reading on the benefits of exercise. Again, there has been lots of scientific research on this.

OPEN

What is your name and three things you are grateful for? If you have been practicing, this should be easier than it was a week ago.

DIG

1. What have you read in your Quiet Time that has blessed you?

Knowing human nature—particularly my own—I have come to realize the importance of accountability in the development of spiritual disciplines. It's like the old business adage: "You get what you inspect, not what you expect." — Ken Hemphill, *The Prayer of Jesus: The Promise and Power of Living in the Lord's Prayer* (Nashville: B&H, 2001).

2. **1 Timothy 4.8; 1 Corinthians 6.19 – 20. Does God care about whether or not we exercise, or does He only care about spiritual stuff, like out prayer life?**

Does God care about fitness? Not as much as He cares about your soul. He cares about eternity more than He cares about time. Physical training is not as important as spiritual training. Running is not as important as reading the Word. Working out is not as important as praying.

But it is important. The Bible says so: "For physical training is of some value, but godliness has value for all things, holding promise for both the present life and the life to come." 1 Timothy 4:8 (NIV)

The Bible says that Jesus didn't just grow spiritually. He grew, "in wisdom and stature, and in favor with God and men." Luke 2:52 (NIV). He grew wise. He grew physically. He grew spiritually. He grew socially, or relationally. He grew in a balanced way. Do you want to be like Jesus? Grow in wisdom. Grow spiritually. Grow socially and relationally. And, grow in terms of fitness.

John prayed that his friend would enjoy good health (3 John 1.2) He is clearly not talking about spiritual health because in the next line he says, "even as your soul is getting along well."

Physical health is of medium importance. It is not as important as your soul, but it still matters. — Josh Hunt, *Fat Is Normal; Be Weird* (2015, 2020 Vision).

3. **Why is it not enough just to worry with our souls? Why is it important that we take care of our bodies as well?**

The body is the physical container for the soul and spirit. God's Word clearly establishes that caring for the body is critical to our well-being and our life with God. The apostle Paul affirmed this when he wrote, "Do you not know that your bodies are temples of the Holy Spirit, who is in you, whom you have received from God? You are not your own; you were bought at a price. Therefore honor God with your bodies" (1 Corinthians 6:19–20).

Spirit, soul, and body encompass the totality of the human experience. God designed all three parts of us to work together in harmony and health. As children of God, we are called to be the best we can be and bring glory to our Creator. And God miraculously equips us to do this: "His divine power has given us everything we need for a godly life through our knowledge of him who called us by his own glory and goodness. Through these he has given us his very great and precious promises, so that through them you may participate in the divine nature, having escaped the corruption in the world caused by evil desires" (2 Peter 1:3–4).

When we accept our new life in Christ and our godly nature, we want to submit to the Lord and follow his ways. We submit our will to his will and we develop the deep and abiding trust children have for their Father. — Susan Gregory and Richard J. Bloomer, *The Daniel Cure: The Daniel Fast Way to Vibrant Health* (Grand Rapids, MI: Zondervan, 2013).

4. **Would you say churches tend to concern themselves too much or too little with matters of physical health?**

 Churches tend to concern themselves exclusively with spiritual health. We create Christians who think godliness has to do with how often you read your Bible and nothing to do with how often you run.

The Bible says, "Do you not know that your body is a temple of the Holy Spirit, who is in you, whom you have received from God? You are not your own; you were bought at a price. Therefore honor God with your body." 1 Corinthians 6:19-20 (NIV). What does it mean to honor God with your body? It means to be sexually pure. It means to not gossip with your tongue. It means to not get drunk with wine. It means to not smoke. And, it means to stay fit.

When was the last time you heard a sermon on gluttony? When was the last time you heard one of these verses mentioned in a Bible study?

- Their destiny is destruction, their god is their stomach, and their glory is in their shame. Their mind is on earthly things. Philippians 3:19 (NIV)

- Do not join those who drink too much wine or gorge themselves on meat, for drunkards and gluttons become poor, and drowsiness clothes them in rags. Proverbs 23:20-21 (NIV)

- The one who keeps the law is a son with understanding, but a companion of gluttons shames his father. Proverbs 28:7 (ESV)

Being fit is not the only thing. It is not the most important thing. It is a lesser thing. And, it is always difficult to pay enough attention to second and third priorities. We can get ramped up about getting first things first. Third or fourth priorities still need to be done. Don't ignore them altogether.

We can make two mistakes with reference to health— we can make it centrally important and make fitness our God. Or, we can ignore it altogether. For twenty years, I ignored it all together. Fifty pounds later, it is time to repent. That is the topic of the next chapter. — Josh Hunt, *Fat Is Normal; Be Weird* (2015, 2020 Vision).

5. **Would you guess church-goers are more or less healthy than average?**

    Maybe it's all the church socials, but a new study finds that those who attend religious activities are more likely to gain weight than those who don't go to church as often.

    Religious involvement is linked to many positive health outcomes, such as happiness, lower rates of smoking and alcohol use, and even a longer life. But research has also suggested that middle-aged adults who are more religious are more likely to be obese. Past data have noted only a correlation between religiosity and weight gain, however; they did not show whether participating in religious activities leads to weight gain, or whether overweight individuals are more likely to seek support in their faith. http://healthland.time.com/2011/03/24/why-going-to-church-can-make-you-fat/

6. **1 Timothy 4.8 says that physical training is of some value. What value is it to train yourself physically?**

    A 2012 study in the journal PLOS Medicine showed that 2.5 hours of moderate exercise per week (that's half an hour of brisk walking a day for 5 days) increased life expectancy by 3.5 years.

    But a lot of good research has shown that low fitness is a bigger predictor of premature death, no matter how much you weigh.

    Low fitness stood out by far as the single strongest predictor of death—more powerful even than obesity, diabetes, high cholesterol, high blood pressure, and smoking.

It wasn't even close. In fact, the research shows that if you're highly fit when in your eighties, you're less likely to die than if you're unfit when in your sixties.

That means if you're a middle-aged, obese smoker with high blood pressure, high cholesterol, and diabetes, the single best thing you can do to improve your health is exercise. — Josh Hunt, *Fat Is Normal; Be Weird* (2015, 2020 Vision).

7. **What exactly is meant by** *training* **in this context?**

Discipline is from gumnazō, from which our English words "gymnasium" and "gymnastics" derive. It means "to train," or "to exercise." The word speaks of the rigorous, strenuous, self-sacrificing training an athlete undergoes.

Every Greek city had its gymnasium, and Ephesus was no exception. Youths customarily spent much of their time from ages sixteen to eighteen in physical training. That was vital, since life in those days involved much physical activity. There was a great emphasis on physical training and the glory of winning athletic events.

By using gumnazō, Paul plays off that cultural phenomenon and applies it to the spiritual realm. — John F. MacArthur Jr., *1 Timothy, MacArthur New Testament Commentary* (Chicago: Moody Press, 1995), 163.

8. **Why do you want to devote yourself to physical training? What motivation do you have for taking care of your body?**

In order to get and stay healthy, it is critical for you to know why it is important. What drives your desire to be healthy?

Is it because it is God's will for you to take care of your body? Consider 1 Corinthians 6:19 – 20: "Do you not know that your bodies are temples of the Holy Spirit, who is in you, whom you have received from God? You are not your own; you were bought at a price. Therefore honor God with your bodies."

Is it because you are in pain or tired of feeling sick, lethargic, forgetful, and not anywhere near your best?

"God is always more interested in why we do something than in what we do. Attitudes count more than achievements." — Pastor Warren

Is it because you want to feel healthy and vibrant to live out your purpose, to do the work you love, to be with the people you care about, or to see your grandchildren grow up?

Is it because you want to prevent illnesses that may run in your family, such as diabetes, cancer, heart disease, or Alzheimer's disease?

Write down your motivation — why it is important for you to get healthy — and then look at it daily. We find it most effective if you approach it from two perspectives: To attain benefits, and to avoid negative consequences. — Rick Warren, Daniel Amen, and Mark Hyman, *The Daniel Plan: 40 Days to a Healthier Life* (Grand Rapids, MI: Zondervan, 2013).

9. **Same two questions we have asked before: first, what good things come to those who regularly exercise?**

The value of mental-training games may be speculative, as Dan Hurley writes in his article on the quest to make ourselves smarter, but there is another, easy-to-achieve, scientifically proven way to make yourself smarter. Go for a walk or a swim. For more than a decade, neuroscientists and physiologists have been gathering evidence of the beneficial relationship between exercise and brainpower. But the newest findings make it clear that this isn't just a relationship; it is the relationship. Using sophisticated technologies to examine the workings of individual neurons — and the makeup of brain matter itself — scientists in just the past few months have discovered that exercise appears to build a brain that resists physical shrinkage and enhance cognitive flexibility. Exercise, the latest neuroscience suggests, does more to bolster thinking than thinking does. http://www.nytimes.com/2012/04/22/magazine/how-exercise-could-lead-to-a-better-brain.html?_r=0

10. **What price do the couch potatoes pay?**

Whether we're fully conscious of it or not, we're always looking for how to be happy. And exercise is one of the most obvious steps to take, as it's not a coincidence that you feel better after a good workout: It's science. A Penn State University study found that people who exercised, whether it was a mild, moderate or vigorous workout, had more pleasant feelings than those who didn't.

These same people were also happier on days when they were more physically active than usual, meaning that upping the ante on workouts can provide even more of a happiness boost. The takeaway? Working out can make you happy long term; adding extra intensity can make you feel even better.

Another experiment used a smartphone app to have participants track their activity, location and happiness levels throughout the day. It received more than 3 million responses a year — and users were at their second-happiest post-workout. https://draxe.com/benefits-of-exercise/

11. **Let's make a long list of things we could do to exercise. We made a similar list last week with ways to serve. We are not committing to anything. Just make a long list.**

My two favorites: tennis and walking.

12. **Every January millions of people sign up for the gym. How long would you guess it takes before the quit going?**

12% of new gym memberships come in January come by percentage, but it actually represents about a 33-50% increase in volume. The second week of January is almost always the busiest of the year.

80% of the New Years Resolutions crowd drops off by the second week of February. Meaning only 20% remain, and the rate of sign-ups tapers off by February (almost all of that initial spike, save for maybe 1-2% of total volume for the year.) https://www.quora.com/What-percentage-of-new-gym-members-in-January-stop-coming-after-February

13. Why do you think they stop going? Why pay the money and then not go? They are clearly motivated or they would not have signed up. Why do you think they stop?

Many of us have these great expectations of getting in shape just in time for the warmer weather. Who wouldn't want to look great in her new bathing suit? As a result, thousands of people join the gym for a "New Year's resolution." But by mid-February, the flocks of people who were hoarding the machines vanish. What are the reasons for abandoning the gym, and how can we do a better job staying on track with our goals? Here are some reasons we quit the gym.

Time constraints. The thought of waking up early to exercise before work can seem rather daunting. Because really, who doesn't love that extra hour of sleep? However, even after a long day at work, hitting the gym still doesn't seem too appealing. With a million other things to check off our to-do lists, the gym can easily be pushed aside and turn into an aspiration of tomorrow. Instead we figure out what to make for dinner or what to grab at the store on our way home.

Expenses. Things cost money, plain and simple. Many people don't want to pay for a gym membership if they're not going that often. It could be too expensive to join, or maybe they feel as if they're draining money by not going. Regardless, money is probably one of the most relevant reasons people quit the gym.

Prolonged results. Sometimes when we don't see results right away, we begin to lose motivation and purpose. Humans tend to want immediate gratification, and it can be irritating when we don't see it in one of those many mirrors on the wall. (It's important to note that we are still doing our bodies a tremendous favor by exercising.)

Read more at http://womensrunning.competitor.com/2016/03/health-wellness/why-people-quit-the-gym_56438#8WGsUr2b0urEopmZ.99

14. **We made a list of possible forms of exercise. Which do you think would best work for you over the long run?**

Like diets, exercise trends come and go. From Zumba classes to CrossFit, it seems like there are endless types workouts tailored for different levels of physical ability. But are these workouts really helping you get healthy or are they just all hype? And which kind is the best for overall health?

When it comes to the best form of exercise, experts say good old-fashion walking is the best.

"Walking is a superfood. It's the defining movement of a human," says Katy Bowman, a biomechanist based in Ventura, California. "It's a lot easier to get movement than it is to get exercise."

While other forms of exercise build endurance and burn fat, these health benefits mean nothing if people are sedentary before and after a workout.

"Actively sedentary is a new category of people who are fit for one hour but sitting around the rest of the day," Bowman says. "You can't offset 10 hours of stillness with one hour of exercise."

- See more at: http://www.techtimes.com/articles/16732/20140929/what-best-form-exercise-experts-walk.htm#sthash.vCYe2GSw.dpuf

15. **Let's talk a little about food. Do you think God cares what we eat? Or, does He only care about whether or not we pray?**

Christians should be the most healthy people group, especially when we consider the physical condition of Jesus Christ, our Founder and Leader. Carole Lewis is an author and the director of a successful weight-loss program called "First Place 4 Health," so-called because as Christians, we are to give Christ first place in our lives and that means in all things, even what we put in our mouths. She said, "The pictures of Jesus that I remember from my childhood showed Him to be rather frail; however, the Jesus of the Scriptures is quite a different person. We know that Jesus was a carpenter by trade. Until He began His public ministry at age 30, He earned His living as a carpenter. He had to carry large pieces of wood and stone to build structures. His trade required great physical strength. We also know from Scripture that Jesus walked from Sidon to Tyre, which would have been a 40-mile trip [that He could have walked] in one day."

When God spoke to me about my weight, I finally faced my situation. I took the first step. I decided to go to the Bible for help. Philippians 1:20-21 says, "Christ will be magnified in my body, whether by life or by death. For to me, to live is Christ, and to die is gain." Christ wanted to be magnified in my body! That was amazing! I'm a Christian, and "Christian" means "little Christ." In other words, we are to be Christ-like. Our Leader—Jesus Christ—was in such great physical condition that He could walk 40 miles, not in Reeboks but in leather sandals; and yet His followers on this planet are unhealthy, overweight, sedentary couch potatoes. That concerns me, and it ought to concern you. God wants to address this condition not only in our bodies but in our churches as well. God wants to help us in this area of weight management. — *Bod 4 God: The Four Keys to Weight Loss* by Steve Reynolds

16. What are some simple steps we could all take to improve our health by improving what we eat? Let's make a long list.

• Instead of a bagel, I eat a protein health bar • Instead of ice cream, I eat nonfat yogurt • Instead of diet sodas, I drink water during the day • I went from eating no fruit to eating an apple a day • I went from eating a hamburger and fries to eating chicken salad with a small amount of lowfat dressing • Instead of using mayonnaise on sandwiches, I use mustard • Instead of fried chips and dip, I eat baked chips and salsa • Instead of eating lots of beef, I eat lots of chicken and some fish • Instead of white bread, I eat whole-grain bread • Instead of fried foods, I eat baked foods (reduces the amount of fat) • Instead of vegetable oil, I use olive oil (a monounsaturated oil—the good kind of fat!) • Instead of high-fat creamer, I use fat-free creamer — *Bod 4 God: The Four Keys to Weight Loss* by Steve Reynolds

17. Without getting too deep in the weeds, what have you learned about eating healthfully?

I was talking to a friend the other day about a book I am reading — Why We Get Fat and What to Do About It, by Gary Taubes. It is one of the most well-documented, well-researched books on the subject. He says that carbs—by which he means bad carbs, (things like potatoes and pasta and sweets), should be thought of like poison. They have no nutritional value whatsoever and can do you a good deal of harm. His words:

> Carbohydrate withdrawal is often interpreted as a 'need for carbohydrate,' " says Westman. "It's like

telling smokers who are trying to quit that their withdrawal symptoms are caused by a 'need for cigarettes' and then suggesting they go back to smoking to solve the problem.

Did you get that? Carbs are like cigarettes. At least, bad carbs are.

Anyway, I was telling my friend this and he said he disagreed. He said he thought we need a balanced diet and eliminating one food group just didn't sound right.

My darker self wanted to ask a series of questions:

- How much research have you done on this?

- How many books have you read?

- How is your weight loss plan going? (My friend could stand to lose some pounds.)

The conversation got me thinking about the whole notion of a balanced diet. I think it is a dangerous concept. We can take balanced to mean almost anything. We can put all kinds of garbage in our diet in the name of balance.

The research is pretty clear. You don't need bad carbs to balance your diet. Bad carbs are anything white:

- Wheat

- Sugar

Let me stop there. That covers a lot of territory. If you eliminated these two things you would almost certainly lose weight. Three more:

- Potatoes

- Rice

- Corn

All of these foods have a high glycemic index, meaning they turn to sugar very quickly. This raises insulin levels and causes you to get fat.

You don't need any of these at all. You may want them. They might taste good. You might choose to eat them. They won't kill you, at least not if you don't eat much of them. But, don't justify eating them in the name of a balanced diet. Justify eating them in the name of, "They just taste good and I want some. — Josh Hunt, *Fat Is Normal; Be Weird* (2015, 2020 Vision).

18. How can our spiritual walk help us live healthier lives?

First, it means that God's Spirit is a resident in your life. The Scripture assumes that the moment you come to Christ—the moment you were saved—the Holy Spirit came into your life. Jesus said, "I will pray the Father, and He will give you another Helper, that He may abide with you forever—the Spirit of truth, whom the world cannot receive, because it neither sees Him nor knows Him; but you know Him, for He dwells with you and will be in you" (John 14:16-17). God lives in you. Think about it; you as a Christian actually house deity. God doesn't live in a church building. There is nothing sacred about a church building except that it is a place where we come together to corporately worship the Lord. Our bodies are sacred because they are God's temples. Second, it means that we are to reflect the glory of God. In 1 Corinthians 6:20, Paul says, "For you were bought with a price, therefore glorify God in your body." Because my body is His temple, I should treat it accordingly. In 1 Corinthians 10:31, Paul says, "Therefore, whether you eat or drink or whatever you do, do all to the glory of God." The Bible tells us that one of the ways we can glorify God is through what we eat and what we drink. — *Bod 4 God: The Four Keys to Weight Loss* by Steve Reynolds

19. **What do you want to apply from today's study?**

20. **What are some of your take aways from this study as a whole?**

21. **How can we support one another in prayer this week?**

Made in the USA
Columbia, SC
15 November 2018